STOKE CITY FOOTBALL CLUB: An A-Z

Dean Hayes

Published by Sigma Leisure – an imprint of
Sigma Press, 1 South Oak Lane, Wilmslow, Cheshire SK9 6AR, England.

British Library Cataloguing in Publication Data
A CIP record for this book is available from the British Library.

ISBN: 1-85058-570-9

Typesetting and Design by: Sigma Press, Wilmslow, Cheshire.

Printed by: MFP Design & Print

Cover Design: The Agency, Wilmslow

Photographs: kindly supplied by Peter Stafford, Wade Martin, F. Perry and Smith Davis Press.

Acknowledgments: The author wishes to thank the following in producing this book: Ben Hayes, Keith Macbeth, David Brunt, Mark Oliver and, finally, Graham Beech of Sigma Press for his support in producing books in this A-Z series.

T h e   A   –   Z

ABANDONED MATCHES

An abandoned match may be defined as one which is called off by the referee whilst it is in progress because conditions do not permit it to be completed. Far fewer matches are abandoned in modern times because if there is some doubt about the ability to play the full game, the match is more likely to be postponed.

Under the early rules of the game, time lost when a match was abandoned had to be replayed at a later date. This led to some very curious meetings. During the 1988-89 season, Stoke and Wolverhampton met for just five minutes – followed by a full-length friendly to placate spectators!

On 25th November 1922, Stoke's train from Preston to Blackburn was delayed due to a hold-up further down the line. Two taxis arrived, but one of these, carrying half the team, broke down. The match at Ewood Park finally started some thirty minutes late and was duly abandoned with Rovers 1-0 up and just four minutes of time remaining. Stoke were fined £25 and to make matters worse, lost the replayed match 5-1.

Below is a list of abandoned League and Cup matches involving the Potters:

Date	Opponents	Competition	Venue	Score
23.11.1889	Notts. County	Football League	Home	2-2
2.12.1911	Queen's Park Rangers	Southern League	Home	0-2*
16.1.1913	Reading	FA Cup	Home	2-2
25.11.1922	Blackburn Rovers	Division One	Away	0-1
11.1.1930	Doncaster Rovers	FA Cup	Away	3-2
15.3.1947	Aston Villa	Division One	Away	2-2
2.1.1954	West Ham United	Division Two	Away	1-4
3.12.1960	Liverpool	Division Two	Home	0-0
22.12.1962	Swansea Town	Division Two	Home	0-0
6.1.1979	Oldham Athletic	FA Cup	Home	2-0

* Result made to stand.

ACCRINGTON

A different club from the Accrington Stanley which joined the League in 1921. Accrington were founder members of the League in 1888, and resigned in 1893 after being relegated to the Second Division. The two clubs first met on 29th September 1888 when Stoke lost 4-2 at home. Accrington completed the double over the Potters, winning the return match 2-0. Stoke gained revenge the following season with a 7-1 victory, with Bob Ramsey scoring a hat-trick – the club's first in the League. The two clubs last met on Boxing Day 1892 when Accrington won 5-2. The Lancashire club are the only founder members of the League no longer in membership.

ACCRINGTON STANLEY

They joined the League as founder members of the Third Division (North) in 1921-22 and spent a total of 33 full seasons as members. A financial crisis finally forced them to withdraw from the League on 6th March 1962 and their record was expunged. Stoke met Accrington Stanley only in the 1926-27 season when the Potters won both games 1-0.

AGE

Youngest

The youngest player to appear in a Football League fixture for Stoke City was Peter Bullock, an England schoolboy international. He made his league debut in the match against Swansea at Vetch Field on 19th April 1958 when he was just 16 years 153 days old. He scored the Potters' goal in a 4-1 defeat.

Oldest

The oldest player to line up in a City first team was Stanley Matthews. He was 50 years 5 days old when he last turned out for the club. The match was against Fulham at the Victoria Ground on 6th February 1965. Stoke won the game 3-1.

ALLEN, TONY

Arriving at the Victoria Ground from Wellington Road School, he made his Stoke debut in a 1-0 win at Doncaster Rovers on 14th September 1957.

An England Youth international, he won a full England cap before he was 20 when he played against Sweden in the 1959-60 season. In total he won 3 full caps, 7 England Under-23 caps and made two appearances for the Football League.

Tony Allen: An England international who played in 473 first team games for the Potters.

A very stylish full-back, he played an important role during the Matthews revival at the Victoria Ground and the club's consolidation in the top flight. He won a Second Division championship medal in 1962-63 and a League Cup runners-up medal in 1963-64. As he began to lose a little of his pace, he was moved to centre-half, but in early 1970, after 473 first team appearances for Stoke, he was transferred to Bury for £10,000.

After 29 league appearances for the Gigg Lane club, he played in South Africa for Hellenic, and in non-League football for Stafford Rangers.

ANGLO-ITALIAN CUP

When Swindon Town won the Football League Cup in 1969, they were ineligible for the Fairs Cup because they were not a First Division side. Consequently, they organised a match against the Italian League Cup winners, A.S. Roma, playing for the Anglo-Italian League Cup. The following year the Anglo-Italian Cup was introduced for club sides from the two countries who had no involvement in Europe.

Stoke first entered at the end of the 1971-72 season. Their results were:

Cantanzaro	(Home) 2-0	(Away) 3-0	
A.S.Roma	(Home) 1-2	(Away) 0-2	

Stoke next entered the competition when it was reintroduced in 1993-94. Their results were:

Birmingham City	(Home) 2-0	Wolverhampton W.	(Away) 3-3
Cosenza	(Home) 2-1	Padova	(Away) 0-3
Florentina	(Home) 0-0	Pescara	(Away) 1-2

In 1994-95, Stoke reached the semi-final stages of the competition after being unbeaten in their group matches. Both games against Notts. County were goalless before the Meadow Lane club won 3-2 on penalties. Their results were:

Ancona	(Home) 1-1	Cesena	(Away) 2-0
Piacenza	(Home) 4-0	Udinese	(Away) 3-1
Notts. County	(Home) 0-0	Notts. County	(Away) 0-0

The results for 1995-96 were:

Salernitana	(Home) 2-2	Foggia	(Away) 1-1
Brescia	(Home) 1-1		

APPEARANCES

The players with the highest number of appearances for Stoke City FC are as follows:

	F.Lg.	FA Cup	F.Lg. Cup	Total
Eric Skeels	495(12)	42(2)	36(2)	573(16)
John McCue	502	40	-	542
Bob McGrory	479	32	-	511
Tony Allen	414(3)	30	26	470(3)
Denis Smith	406(1)	29	34	469(1)
Alan Bloor	384(4)	38	37	463
Peter Fox	409	22	32	463
Frank Bowyer	398	38	-	436
Frank Mountford	391	34	-	425
Jackie Marsh	346(9)	32	35	422

Five players have made over one hundred consecutive appearances at any time during their careers with Stoke City:

¤ Tony Allen: 121 appearances (17th March 1960 to 27th March 1963)

¤ Arthur Turner: 118 appearances (27th April 1935 to 12th March 1938)

¤ Tom Holford: 105 appearances (14th March 1903 to 17th February 1906)

¤ Alan Dodd: 102 appearances (10th January 1976 to 29th April 1978)

¤ Bob McGrory: 101 appearances (27th March 1926 to 29th September 1928)

ASHINGTON

Ashington were members of the Third Division (North) for its first eight seasons 1921 to 1929. In 1929 they failed to gain re-election. The two clubs met in the 1926-27 season when Stoke won the championship. The Potters won 7-0 at the Victoria Ground, with Charlie Wilson scoring five, and 2-0 in the north-east, with goals from Wilson and Eyres.

ASPREY, BILL

A powerfully built defender, his early career at the Victoria Ground was interrupted by National Service. Converted from wing-half to full-back, he went on to make 341 appearances for the club. He showed his versatility when asked by managers Taylor and Waddington to play in attack when there was either a shortage of goals or strikers. This did pay dividends. He scored two in the club's 9-0 victory over Plymouth, and a hat-trick in the 5-3 win over Charlton Athletic.

In 1966 he joined Oldham Athletic and later played for Port Vale before moving into coaching and management. He was assistant-manager to Noel Cantwell at Coventry City; coach to Sheffield Wednesday, Wolves and West Bromwich Albion; and manager of

Oxford United. Subsequently, F joined Stoke in February 1982 ἑ assistant-manager to Richie Barker.

Following Barker's dismissal, Asprey took over, though initially as caretaker boss. During this time he inspired a revival and Stoke just managed to avoid relegation. He was then appointed permanently to the post, but with little money to spend, the club finished rock bottom of the First Division in 1984-85 with their lowest goals and points totals ever. The season affected Asprey's health and it came as no surprise when he left.

Stoke City's full League record under Bill Asprey was:

Bill Asprey: Wolverhampton-born defender who went on to manage the club before ill-health forced him to leave.

P.	W.	D.	L.	F.	A.
67	14	13	40	50	121

ATTENDANCES AT THE VICTORIA GROUND

Attendance figures at home provide some interesting statistics:

Individual Matches: Highest in the Football League

Opponents	Date	Competition	Attendance
Arsenal	29.3.1937	Division One	51,380
Blackpool	27.12.1947	Division One	47,609
Port Vale	4.9.1954	Division Two	47,000
Liverpool	31.3.1975	Division One	45,954
Manchester United	16.10.1948	Division One	45,830
Manchester United	18.4.1964	Division One	45,697
Arsenal	28.9.1935	Division One	45,470
Arsenal	6.10.1934	Division One	45,349
Wolverhampton Wanderers	26.10.1946	Division One	45,000
Arsenal	7.2.1948	Division One	45,000

Other games at the Victoria Ground

Bolton Wanderers	2.3.1946	FA Cup Rd 6	50,735
Blackburn Rovers	27.1.1962	FA Cup Rd 4	49,486
Manchester United	22.3.1972	FA Cup Rd 6 (R)	49,091
Port Vale	6.1.1951	FA Cup Rd 3	48,000
West Ham United	29.1.1951	FA Cup Rd 4	47,929
Tottenham Hotspur	7.1.1950	FA Cup Rd 3	47,000
Hull City	12.2.1949	FA Cup Rd 5	46,738
Aston Villa	4.1.1958	FA Cup Rd 3	45,800
Blackpool	29.1.1949	FA Cup Rd 4	45,000
Aston Villa	18.2.1922	FA Cup Rd 3	43,689

Stoke City's average home league attendances over the last ten years have been as follows:

1986-87	9,987	1991-92	13,007
1987-88	9,607	1992-93	16,589
1988-89	9,817	1993-94	15,964
1989-90	12,449	1994-95	12,910
1990-91	11,565	1995-96	12,266

¤　The club's overall best season's average was 31,590 in 1947-48.

¤　The club's lowest season's average was 3,275 in 1889-90.

¤　The club's lowest home attendance was 1,000 for the match against Newton Heath on 7th January 1893.

¤　The club's lowest home attendance since 1946 was 4,070 for the match against Ipswich Town on 30th March 1960.

A crowd of 84,569 crammed into Maine Road to watch the Manchester City v Stoke City FA Cup tie on 3rd March 1934. The crowd was the largest for any cup-tie at a club game outside London and Glasgow.

AUSTERBERRY, HORACE

Horace Austerberry spent eleven seasons in charge at the Victoria Ground, the first ten of which saw the club playing in the top flight.

An assistant schoolmaster to Tom Slaney at St John's School in Hanley, he was invited by the former secretary-manager to watch Stoke play and then report on the game as a journalist. Taking over from William Rowley as manager in September 1897, he was a strict disciplinarian and once suspended three players for drinking champagne in breach of club rules.

After being relegated in 1907, the club suffered a financial crisis in 1908 and he left the game to go into journalism.

Stoke's full League record under Horace Austerberry was:

P.	W.	D.	L.	F.	A.
382	134	77	171	502	592

AUTOGLASS TROPHY

The Autoglass Trophy replaced the Leyland Daf Cup for the 1991-92 season.

After qualifying from their group with wins over Walsall (away 2-0) and Birmingham City (home 3-1), the Potters then disposed of Cardiff City (home 3-0), Walsall again (home 3-1) and Leyton Orient (away 1-0) before playing Peterborough United in the Southern Area Final. After being held to a 3-3 draw at the Victoria Ground, it was Paul Ware's superb goal that decided the clash and took Stoke to Wembley. The Potters won the Autoglass Trophy at the expense of Stockport County, with Mark Stein scoring the winner in front of 48,000 fans (34,000 of them wearing the red and white of Stoke).

In 1992-93, the club won through to the Area semi-final, only to lose 1-0 at home to rivals Port Vale.

AWAY GAMES

Best Away Wins

Opponents:	Date:	Competition:	Score:
Bury	13.3.1954	Division Two	6-0
Wrexham	26.2.1927	Division 3 (N)	6-2
Bristol City	1.2.1930	Division Two	6-2
Southampton	27.8.1927	Division Two	6-3
Birmingham City	21.9.1935	Division One	5-0
Blackburn Rovers	22.1.1923	Division One	5-1
Fulham	12.11.1927	Division Two	5-1
Nottingham Forest	25.8.1928	Division Two	5-1
Wigan Borough	9.1.1926	FA Cup Rd 3	5-2
Chelsea	12.10.1946	Division One	5-2

**Mark Stein, scorer of the winning goal at Wembley in 1992 when Stoke beat
Stockport County 1-0.**

Worst Away Defeats

Preston North End	14.9.1889	Football Lg	0-10
Darwen	3.10.1891	Football Lg	3-9
Everton	2.11.1889	Football Lg	0-8
Blackburn Rovers	4.1.1890	Football Lg	0-8
Wolverhampton Wanderers	22.2.1890	FA Cup Q Rd 3	0-8
Preston North End	6.10.1888	Football Lg	0-7
Liverpool	4.1.1902	Division One	0-7

Highest Scoring Away Draws

Bolton Wanderers	15.10.1892	Division One	4-4
Charlton Athletic	9.9.1929	Division Two	4-4
Cardiff City	21.11.1959	Division Two	4-4

¤ Most Away Wins in a Season: 12 in 1932-33 (Division Two)

¤ Fewest Away Wins in a Season: 0 in 1891-92 (Football League)
                                      0 in 1893-94 (Division One)
                                      0 in 1897-98 (Division One)
                                      0 in 1968-69 (Division One)
                                      0 in 1984-85 (Division One)

¤ Most Away Defeats in a Season: 17 in 1922-23 (Division One)

¤ Fewest Away Defeats in a Season: 3 in 1978-79 (Division Two)

¤ Most Away Goals in a Season: 38 in 1932-33 (Division Two)

¤ Fewest Away Goals in a Season: 6 in 1984-85 (Division One)

B

BALL, ALAN

Playing a major role in England's 1966 World Cup triumph, Alan Ball's tremendous work-rate was an inspiration for his team-mates and he went on to win 72 caps. The Farnworth-born midfielder's transfers broke the British record twice. When he joined Everton from Blackpool in 1966, he cost £110,000, and when he moved from Everton to Arsenal in 1971, he cost a new record £220,000 fee.

He won a League championship medal with Everton in 1969-70, and ended on the losing side in two FA Cup Finals. After further spells with Southampton, Blackpool and Bristol Rovers, he retired in 1984 with 743 League appearances to his name.

In May of that year he took over as manager of Portsmouth, leading them into the First Division in 1987. Unfortunately, the Fratton Park side were relegated the following season, and in January 1989 he was sacked. After a short spell as Jock Wallace's assistant at Colchester, he moved to Stoke in a similar capacity.

After his appointment as manager, the club slipped down the Second Division and were relegated to the Third Division for the first time since 1927. In February 1991, after a 4-0 defeat at Wigan Athletic when Ball alleged that a young fan had abused him, he resigned. Appointed manager of Exeter City in August 1991, he moved to Southampton before taking over as manager of Manchester City in July 1995. After a poor start to the 1995-96 campaign, City lost their Premiership status on the last day of the season and Alan Ball resigned in August 1996.

Stoke City's full League record under Alan Ball was:

P.	W.	D.	L.	F.	A.
58	15	20	23	58	69

BANKS, GORDON

Joining Leicester City after just one year with Chesterfield, he became one of the first goalkeepers to attract a large transfer fee when he moved from Filbert Street to Stoke City for £52,000 in April 1967. His departure from Leicester came about because, amazingly, the club unearthed another goalkeeper of similar potential in Peter Shilton!

Banks is arguably the greatest goalkeeper of all time and the save he made from Pele in the 1970 World Cup in Mexico is claimed to be the best ever save. People still talk about the Brazilian's downward header, Banks's anticipation of the bounce and his full stretch dive to somehow scoop the ball from under the crossbar.

In almost six years at the Victoria Ground, he made 246 first team appearances and kept 71 clean sheets. A fixture in the England side, he made 36 of his 73 appearances whilst with Stoke. In 1972 he was voted Footballer of the Year. His contribution at Wembley that year was immense – when Stoke won the League Cup against Chelsea, he was in outstanding form.

Sadly, on 22nd October 1972, whilst returning home from the Victoria Ground after treatment, he was involved in a road crash that was to cost him the sight of his right eye. So highly was he regarded that television companies interrupted their programmes to advise of his accident and progress. Though he played with great distinction for a couple of seasons with NASL side Fort Lauderdale Strikers, he was unable to regain his place in the Stoke side.

After retiring from the game, he coached at Stoke and at Port Vale as well as managing Telford United. The most likeable of men, Gordon Banks was simply the best.

BARKER, ALFRED

Appointed secretary-manager of Stoke Football Club (1908) Limited, his first job was to add the club's name to the list seeking to enter the Football League. Having only just lost their status, the club was eliminated in the first round after polling just six of the thirty votes cast.

A former League referee, he was not disheartened and set about rebuilding the club. Joining the Birmingham and District League, the Stoke side acquitted themselves well against strong reserve sides of the top Midland clubs.

He remained in office for six years until April 1914 when he resigned, following his omission to seek exemption for the club from the preliminary rounds of the FA Cup. It was a sad ending for a man who did much to save the game of football within the city.

BARKER, RICHIE

Richie Barker was an experienced non-League player when he entered League football with Derby County at the age of 28. He made 11 appearances in Derby's Second Division championship season of 1968-69, but was transferred to Notts. County midway through that campaign. He helped County win the Fourth Division title in 1970-71, but after breaking his leg whilst playing for Peterborough, he moved into management as assistant to his former Derby colleague, Alan

Durban at Shrewsbury Town. They combined to take the Gay Meadow club from the Fourth to the Second Division and when the Welshman moved to Stoke City, Barker took control at Shrewsbury. Ten months later he moved to Wolves as assistant-manager.

Moving to Stoke in June 1981, he had disagreements with players Mike Doyle and Ray Evans, and also sold Adrian Heath to Everton for £700,000. Gradually, however, he won the fans' backing when he signed midfielders Sammy McIlroy and Mickey Thomas, as well as Mark Chamberlain from Port Vale. But, after a disastrous start to the 1983-84 season, he was sacked. He had attempted to convert Stoke to a long-ball game and the players never came to terms with it.

He returned to Notts. County, but after a poor season he was replaced. After working in Greece and Egypt, he returned to England as Ron Atkinson's assistant at Sheffield Wednesday.

Stoke City's full League record under Richie Barker was:

P.	W.	D.	L.	F.	A.
101	30	23	48	109	160

BARROW

They joined the League upon the formation of the Third Division (North) and were promoted for the only time in their history in 1966-67 when they moved from the Fourth to the Third Division.

The two clubs met only in the 1926-27 season when a Charlie Wilson hat-trick helped Stoke to a 4-0 home win on 16th October 1926. The return fixture saw the Potters play out a goalless draw.

In 1972, after previously surviving ten re-election applications, they were voted out of the League and replaced by Hereford United.

BEST STARTS

City were unbeaten for the first nine games of the 1926-27 league season in the Third Division (North). Ending the season as champions, their record before losing 5-0 at New Brighton on 2nd October was:

P.	W.	D.	L.	F.	A.
9	7	2	0	24	4

BIGGEST DEFEAT

The club's biggest defeat in the Football League occurred on Saturday 14th September, 1889 when they were hammered 10-0 by Preston North End at Deepdale. It was reported that Jimmy Ross scored seven of the goals for the winners that day.

BIGGEST WINS

The club's first FA Cup win was on 30th October 1886 when they beat Caernarfon Wanderers 10-1, yet statisticians persist in naming Stoke's 10-3 win over West Bromwich Albion in 1936-37 as 'the biggest win'. It is, of course, in the Football League.

Yet in 1877-78, when Stoke were the first winners of the Staffordshire County Cup, they beat Mow Cop 26-0 in an earlier round – a record for all competitions that will surely never be beaten!

BIRMINGHAM LEAGUE

Stoke entered their first team in the Birmingham and District League for the 1909-10 season, only to find it dominated by the reserve sides of Aston Villa, Crewe Alexandra and Wolves. Stoke ended the season in seventh place, with Hartshill-born Arthur Griffiths top-scoring with 36 League goals in 42 appearances. He scored two hat-tricks and scored twice on no less than eleven occasions. When the Potters entertained West Bromwich Albion, they scored before a West Brom player touched the ball, but eventually lost 3-1.

The following season saw Stoke as champions of the Birmingham League, beating Halesowen 10-0 in the process. At the end of that highly successful campaign, the club's directors decided that for the 1911-12 season, they should leave the Birmingham League to the Reserves and concentrate on the First Division of the Southern League.

BLOOR, ALAN

As a schoolboy, Alan Bloor was always acknowledged to be an outstanding talent, both at Uttoxeter Road CP and the Queensbury Road School. Playing for the Stoke-on-Trent Schoolboys, he accepted

Alan Bloor: A resolute defender who completed 18 seasons at the Victoria Ground.

apprentice forms at City before winning an England Youth international cap. He, in fact, captained his country at that level.

He became a full professional on his 17th birthday, but Tony Waddington refused to rush him and 'Bluto' had to wait until he was 21 before he held a regular first team spot. Forming a partnership with another Queensbury Road boy Denis Smith, he went on to complete 18 seasons at the Victoria Ground. A resolute defender, being both calm and undemonstrative, he was the perfect foil to Smith. The holder of a 1972 Wembley winners' medal in the League Cup and a Watney Cup winners' medal from 1973, he was, without doubt, an integral member of a successful Stoke side.

After playing in 463 League and Cup games for the Potters, he moved to Port Vale as first player-youth coach, and then had a short, unhappy spell as manager.

BONFIRE DAY

On 5th November 1910, Stoke's fixture list demanded that they turn out sides in both the Southern League and Birmingham League. The Southern League team that day was really the second team and they had no trouble in beating Chesham Town at home 3-0, with Vic Horrocks grabbing a hat-trick. The Birmingham League match saw Stoke draw 2-2 at Kidderminster Harriers.

BOOKS

Among the books that have been written about Stoke City Football Club are:

"The Official History of Stoke City" by R.D.L. Austerberry and W.J. Foster (published by News Service, 1948)

"Stoke City Football Club – Centenary Handbook 1863-1963" edited by Peter Buxton (published by Pyramid Press)

"A Potter's Tale" by Wade Martin (published by Barracuda, 1988)

"Stoke City Encyclopaedia" by Tony Matthews (published by Lion Press, 1994)

BOWYER, FRANK

A product of Birches Head School, Frank Bowyer joined Stoke at the age of 17, immediately before the outbreak of the Second World War. As the established professionals joined up, young Frank had plenty of opportunities of playing for the Potters during the war period and scored 56 goals in 162 appearances. He had to wait until February 1948 before making his Football League debut in a 2-0 home defeat by Manchester United.

The following season, he was the leading scorer in the First Division for most of the season, ending with 21 goals from his 31 appearances, including a hat-trick in the 3-1 win at Burnley. He won his only representative honour in 1950 when he was selected by the FA to tour Canada. Despite his late start in the game, he went on to make 398 League appearances, and with 137 goals, he is the second highest League scorer in the club's history, just three behind Freddie Steele.

Released by Stoke in 1960, he joined Macclesfield Town.

BRADFORD PARK AVENUE

Park Avenue enjoyed 47 seasons in the League before failing to hold on to their place in 1969-70, after three consecutive seasons at the bottom of the League. They started their career in the Second Division in 1908-09, and in 1914 joined their Bradford neighbours City in the

First Division. They were relegated in 1920-21 and the following season, which was the season they first met Stoke, they suffered the embarrassment of dropping into the Third Division (North). Park Avenue beat Stoke 1-0 at home, but the Potters gained revenge with a 4-2 win in Yorkshire. The honours between the two clubs were even, each winning five matches with four matches drawn. The last game between the two clubs was on 18th February 1933 when Stoke won 4-0, with goals from Harry Sellars, Ware, Liddle and Mawson. Founder members of the Fourth Division in 1958, Park Avenue won promotion just once before their eventual demise.

BRADSHAW, JOSEPH

Joseph Bradshaw replaced Harry Lockett in August 1890, aiming to rival his predecessor in the amount of commitment shown to the Stoke club. In fact, he did extremely well in his first season as the Potters won the Football Alliance and were elected back into the Football League, as it expanded from 12 to 14 clubs. Midway through the 1891-92 season, however, with the team struggling in the lower reaches, he left the club to be replaced by Arthur Reeves.

BROTHERS

Stoke can claim a remarkable ten sets of brothers who have appeared for the club's first team in Football League matches.

The first brothers were Edgar and Harry Mountford who were around in the club's early seasons. Surprisingly, they never appeared together in the same team. Just before the turn of the century came Billy and John Tunnicliffe, followed by Arthur and Adrian Capes. Arthur was an England international known as 'Sailor', but he left for Bristol City eighteen months before his brother Adrian was signed from Burslem Port Vale. The first brothers to appear together in a Stoke side were George and Amos Baddeley. Their first joint appearance was on 2nd March 1907 and the Potters were beaten 3-1 at Sunderland. They played together on 18 occasions.

After the First World War, Stoke signed Tommy Broad from Manchester City for £500, and his brother Jimmy from Millwall for £2500. Jimmy had been coaching Las Palmas in the Canaries.

They both left the club in April 1924, after appearing in the Stoke side together on 79 occasions. Tommy left to join Southampton, whilst Jimmy, who served with 14 clubs, left to coach Barcelona.

The Stoke careers of Arty and Frank Watkin, who scored on his debut, ran back to back, whilst manager Bob McGrory recruited Doug and Jim Westland from Aberdeen. Doug was a goalkeeper and Jim an inside-forward. Though they played in the same Stoke side on only two occasions, the first of these saw Stoke beat West Bromwich Albion 10-3 on 4th February 1937. Derek and Tony Ward, from Longton, made almost a hundred League appearances between them, but were in the same side on just 11 occasions. Derek joined Stockport County, for whom he scored 21 goals in 81 appearances, whilst Terry retired through ill-health and died in 1963.

Mel Pejic made just one appearance for the Potters whilst brother Mike played in 336 League and Cup games and represented England.

Mark and Neville Chamberlain were both signed from neighbours Port Vale by manager Richie Barker. Though Neville had only seven outings in Stoke colours, brother Mark found fame and international honours with England whilst at the Victoria Ground.

C

CAPACITY

The total capacity of the Victoria Ground in the 1995-96 season was 24,255. The breakdown was as follows:

Boothen End Terrace	10,035
Boothen End Paddock	1,740
Boothen Stand	3,033
Butler Street Paddock	870
Butler Street Stand	1,364
Stoke End Paddock	2,754
Stoke End Stand	4,097
Directors' Box	162
Executive Boxes	200

CAPTAINS

Stoke's first captain in the Football League was Tommy Clare, one of the club's first ever professional players. He won four England caps and made one appearance for the Football League.

George Baddeley was a superb wing-half who captained the side from the turn of the century right up to the time when the club went bankrupt in 1908.

George Turner joined Stoke in 1908 when the new club were on the lookout for the best players in the area. He had been a professional athlete when approached by the club, but was immediately made captain and led the side up to the outbreak of war.

Club captain for many years, John Kirton's most productive times were taken away from him by the hostilities. Given his ability and consistency, there is every chance he would be the holder of the Stoke appearance record.

Perhaps the proudest captain in the club's history was Peter Dobing who collected Stoke's first major prize when they won the Football League Cup in 1972.

CENTRAL LEAGUE

The Central League was formed in 1911 by the Northern and Midland giants of the Football League as a reserve team league. The first ever winners were not, however, giants, but Lincoln City – who won it with 48 points out of a possible 64, and then immediately withdrew from the League, never to return.

The League continued even during the First World War when its regional nature enabled it to carry on whilst the Football League was forced into abeyance.

Stoke first entered the competition in 1921-22 and they did not have long to wait before they won the championship in the 1927-28 season.

The club's record that season was:

P.	W.	D.	L.	F.	A.	PTS.
42	24	8	10	104	62	56

From 1982-83 there were two divisions, and at the end of the 1984-85 campaign Stoke were relegated from the First to the Second Division. In 1991-92, the reserves took the Second Division title with the following record:

P.	W.	D.	L.	F.	A.	PTS.
34	25	5	4	93	30	80

They were relegated the following season, but returned to the top flight in 1993-94, after finishing third behind Tranmere Rovers and West Bromwich Albion.

The club's full record in the Central League is:

P.	W.	D.	L.	F.	A.
2774	1037	626	1111	4130	4420

CENTURIES

Goals

There are nine instances of individual players who have scored a hundred or more goals for Stoke City. John Ritchie has the most goals to his credit with 176 strikes in his Stoke career (1963-74). Freddie Steele scored 159 goals between 1934 and 1949. Other century scorers are Frank Bowyer who scored 149 goals, Charlie Wilson (118), Johnny King (113), Harry Oscroft (107), Jimmy Greenhoff (103), Tommy Sale (103) and Harry Davies (101).

Appearances

Whilst no Stoke player has made one hundred consecutive appearances immediately after making their Football League debut, there are five players who have made one hundred or more consecutive appearances during their careers. They are: Tony Allen (121), Arthur Turner (118), Tom Holford (105), Alan Dodd (102) and Bob McGrory (101).

CHAIRMEN

Below is the full list of Stoke City's chairmen:

Mr A. Fleming*	1885-1887	Mr G.W. Taylor	1955-1957
Mr S. Barker	1887-1897	Mr C.T. Salmon	1957-1959
Mr J.T. Fenton	1897-1899	Mr A.A. Henshall	1959-1962
Mr W.A. Cowlishaw	1899-1908	Mr G.W. Taylor	1962-1966
Rev A.E. Hurst	1908-1914	Mr A.A. Henshall	1966-1976
Mr E.B. Reynish	1914-1924	Mr T. Degg	1976-1980
Mr A.J.C. Sherwin	1924-1936	Mr P. Axon	1980-1983
Ald. H. Booth	1936-1951	Mr F. Edwards	1983-1985
Mr T.A. Preece	1951-1952	Mr S. Clubb	1985-1986
Mr E. Henshall	1952-1953	Mr P. Coates	1986-
Mr T.L. Duddell	1953-1955		

* Believed to have taken office in 1885.

CHAMPIONSHIPS

Stoke City have on four occasions won a divisional championship.

1926-27 Third Division (North) Championship

During this successful campaign, Stoke's only home defeat was at the hands of Stockport County (0-1) on 30th October 1926. They won ten matches away from the Victoria Ground, but suffered their worst defeat, 5-0, at New Brighton. They were one of a number of teams who made a first, and in some cases only, visit to the Victoria Ground. Stoke drew 1-1 with New Brighton, but beat Ashington 7-0, Durham City 4-0, Nelson 4-1 and Wigan Borough 2-0.

Charlie Wilson equalled Jimmy Broad's record of 25 League goals whilst Harry Davies bagged 15 as they ended the season five points clear of their nearest rivals.

Their record was:

P.	W.	D.	L.	F.	A.	PTS.
42	27	9	6	92	40	63

1932-33 Second Division Championship

When Stoke won the Second Division championship in 1932-33, they broke numerous records – 25 victories (as many as any side in Divisions One or Two); best goal average in Divisions One and Two; best away record (won 12 drawn 3 lost 6) in Division Two since the Division was extended to 22 teams; and best goals against record (39) of any side in the League.

Their record was:

P.	W.	D.	L.	F.	A.	PTS.
42	25	6	11	78	39	56

1962-63 Second Division Championship

With the return of Stanley Matthews in the previous season proving something of a catalyst, Tony Waddington was more than hopeful of success at the beginning of the season. Yet it was only after a difficult opening, going down 1-0 to Leeds United led by John Charles, drawing one and losing four of the next five, that the side began to settle. On 12th September 1962, a 6-3 home win over Charlton Athletic, with Dennis Viollet netting four of the goals, saw a dramatic transformation. It was 15th December before Stoke lost again.

The adverse weather conditions meant that between Boxing Day and 2nd March, Stoke played no League fixtures. In March 1963, Stoke signed Jimmy McIlroy from Burnley and though he made his debut in a 6-0 defeat at Norwich, it was the genial Irishman who turned the season round. The Potters, with Chelsea and Sunderland, were in a challenging position for promotion.

Over Easter, Stoke drew 0-0 at Roker Park and then won 2-1 in the Easter Monday clash, with Viollet scoring both goals. There then followed three consecutive defeats before a win at Chelsea. After losing at Bury, the game at home to Luton Town became the crucial promotion-winning game. Both teams were ankle deep in mud, but goals by Mudie and Matthews saw the club promoted as champions while the Hatters went down to Division Three.

Stoke's record was:

P.	W.	D.	L.	F.	A.	PTS.
42	20	13	9	73	50	53

1992-93 Second Division Championship

Stoke enjoyed a run of 25 League games without defeat from 5th September 1992 to 20th February 1993, creating a club record. The top scorer was Mark Stein with 26 goals (five of them penalties).

They ended the season with a total of 93 points, three more than runners-up Bolton Wanderers.

Their record was:

P.	W.	D.	L.	F.	A.	PTS.
46	27	12	7	73	34	93

The nearest the club ever came to winning the First Division championship was in 1946-47. In their last League game of the season, Liverpool beat Wolves 2-1 at Molineux and took over from them at the top of the table. Liverpool had 57 points; Wolves had 56.

Manchester United, despite beating Sheffield United 6-2, also finished with 56 points. Liverpool then had to wait until 14th June to see whether Stoke would overhaul them as Stoke had two points less, but a better goal difference and one game to play. The game was at Bramall Lane, where Stoke lost 2-1 to Sheffield United and, hence, finished fourth. That day is the latest date on which the championship of any division has been decided.

CHURCH LAND

There is no doubt that the Church has played an important part in the history of many football clubs, including Stoke. The land from Stoke Church, Church Street, Lonsdale Street and up towards Campbell Road was all glebeland and the Rector, Sir Lovelace Starmer, encouraged many sporting pursuits, including football, cricket and athletics. He also helped to provide Stoke's early grounds on which they played their matches.

The Church's importance was again evident in the early part of this century when the then Rector, Rev. C.H. Simpkinson, continued his support for the Club when he agreed to give a 21-year lease on the ground. This move gave Stoke a valuable asset and helped them decide on further ground improvements.

CITY

In 1925, with the joining together of the towns of the Potteries to form the new corporation of Stoke-on-Trent, the club added 'City' to its title.

CLEAN SHEET

This is the colloquial expression to describe a goalkeeper's performance when he does not concede a goal.

In the Football League, Roger Jones kept 20 clean sheets in 41 appearances when City won promotion from the Second Division in 1978-79. Bob Dixon kept 18 clean sheets from 41 appearances in 1926-27 as Stoke lifted the Third Division (North) championship.

CLEVELAND STOKERS

In the summer of 1966, Stoke played in the U.S. Soccer Association Tourney under the name of Cleveland Stokers. In the States, there was an altercation between Maurice Setters and Calvin Palmer which resulted in the latter player being withdrawn from the Stoke party.

Failing to win any honours, the club's results in the tournament were as follows:

Aberdeen	Won	2-1	ADO The Hague	Won	4-1
Bangu	Lost	1-2	Cagliari	Drew	1-1
Cerro	Lost	1-2	Dundee United	Won	4-1
Glentoran	Drew	0-0	Hibernian	Won	2-0
Sunderland	Lost	1-3	Shamrock Rovers	Won	1-0
			Wolverhampton Wanderers	Drew	0-0

COLOMBIA

The departure of Stoke's Neil Franklin and George Mountford, along with other leading players, on Monday 8th May, 1950, created a major sensation. They were bound for Bogota, Colombia, and were risking suspension by playing outside the aegis of FIFA for Independiente Sante Fe. Franklin had just played his 35th consecutive game for England, and had declined to go with the England party to the 1950 World Cup in Brazil. He had written to the FA saying that he could not possibly leave home during the summer months because of his wife's health.

Stopping off at New York on their way to Bogota, he told reporters that he did not have a contract with the Independiente Sante Fe club, just an agreement to look over the place. The position of head coach was his if he wanted it, with the position of his deputy open to George Mountford. There were reports of inducements to tempt the players – signing-on fees of 20,000 dollars each, plus 1,000 pesos per match; a free house and servants; and also free medical attention for Franklin's wife who was expecting a baby in the August.

The players and their families were given a rapturous welcome as they landed in Bogota. The skills of the Stoke pair were greatly appreciated by the Colombians, particularly as Mountford scored a hat-trick in the first practice game. Their debuts in the Colombian Premier Division came on 14th May when Medallin were beaten 3-2. Mountford made the first two goals and scored the winner – the players leaving the pitch to the cries of, "Long Live Britain." There was no doubt that the two players and their families were treated like royalty. However, within two months Franklin was back and signed for Hull City, never playing another game for Stoke. Mountford completed the season before returning to Stoke after suspension.

COLOURS

Stoke's first game at the Victoria Ground, on Monday 24th September, 1883, was also the first time the club wore 'their new uniforms of flannel shirts with red and white stripes and white knickerbockers'.

Before that they had played in black and blue shirts and white knickerbockers, and then claret shirts and white knickerbockers.

When playing away, their strip was usually white shirts and black knickerbockers.

Just after the Second World War, the club announced a change of strip and played in white shirts and black shorts instead of the customary red and white stripes. In recent years, with the advent of sponsors, the club have sported a variety of colours, but the red and white stripes still remain the most popular.

COMMISSIONAIRE

In 43 years with the club, Fred Bradley never missed a match, yet, surprisingly, he never saw one either! Commissionaire at the Victoria Ground, he remained in the club's employment from August 1924 to May 1967.

CONROY, TERRY

One of the most popular players ever to appear for Stoke City, Terry Conroy joined the club from Glentoran in March 1967 for a fee of

£10,000. He made his League debut early the following season, scoring the winner in a 3-2 home win over Leicester City.

Easily recognisable with his white legs and ginger hair, it took him another season before he became a regular in the Stoke side. Plagued throughout his career by injuries, he had six cartilage operations in his time at the Victoria Ground and recovered from everyone!

The Dublin-born winger became the first Stoke player to represent the Republic of Ireland when he played against Czechoslovakia in 1969-70, the first of his 27 caps.

Terry Conroy: A Republic of Ireland international who scored the opening goal in Stoke's 2-1 League Cup Final win over Chelsea.

In his twelve years at Stoke he made 333 League and Cup appearances, scoring 66 goals, including the opening goal in the 2-1 win over Chelsea at Wembley in 1972. Eventually allowed to leave the Victoria Ground by Alan Durban in 1979, he played for Bulova in Hong Kong before ending his playing days with Crewe Alexandra.

CONSECUTIVE HOME GAMES

Stoke City have been involved in a number of intense sequences of home games in succession. In 1904-05, they played four Football League and two FA Cup games in the period 28th January – 11th March. In 1955-56, they played five Second Division matches in succession at the Victoria Ground between 27th December 1955 and 3rd March 1956. However, during the 1910-11 season, when the club played in the Southern League Division Two and the Birmingham League, the club were involved in a sequence of eight home games in succession, winning all their matches.

Date:	Opponents:	Competition:	Score:
7.11.1910	Croydon Common	Southern League	6-2
12.11.1910	Wrexham	Birmingham League	6-2
14.11.1910	Aberdare	Southern League	1-0
19.11.1910	Worcester City	FA Cup	7-0
26.11.1910	Wolverhampton W. Res.	Birmingham League	6-1
3.12.1910	Lincoln City	FA Cup	4-0
10.12.1910	Crewe Alexandra	Birmingham League	1-0
12.12.1910	Walsall	Southern League	4-0

COX, WALTER

As a Stoke player, Walter Cox had played in the club's first ever FA Cup game when they were beaten 2-1 at home by Manchester in the first qualifying round. He became secretary-manager in 1883, following Slaney's resignation. His reign, however, was only a short one and in April 1884, ten months after taking office, he left to be replaced by Harry Lockett.

CRICKETERS

The only Stoke players who were cricketers of real note were Tom Revill and Arthur Jepson.

Born in Bolsover, Revill made 74 first team appearances for Stoke, scoring 24 goals. He played cricket for Derbyshire between 1913 and 1920, but only scored 231 runs in twenty innings for a batting average of 14.43. Goalkeeper Arthur Jepson was signed from neighbours Port Vale by Bob McGrory for £3,750. An outstanding medium-pace bowler for Nottinghamshire, he took 1,050 wickets between 1938 and

1959 at an average of 29.06 each. He was also a strong right-handed batsman and scored 6,351 runs for an average of 14.34. He also stood as a Test umpire for a number of years.

Another cricketing goalkeeper was Isaac (Ike) Brookes, the Staffordshire County Cricket wicket-keeper. He kept goal for the Potters for the last 12 games of the 1890-91 season. The team was unbeaten during this time and subsequently won the Football Alliance Championship.

Geoff Hurst played county cricket for Essex in 1962 without scoring a run in his two innings, whilst Peter Dobing was with Lancashire as a cricketing hopeful and, indeed, came on as twelfth man in a Roses match against Yorkshire.

CROWD TROUBLE

However unwelcome, crowd disturbances are far from a modern phenomenon at major football matches. Behaviour at the Victoria Ground has usually been of a high standard, and though Stoke supporters are well-renowned for voicing their opinions at suspect referees, the occasions when their demonstrations boil over beyond the verbal are very rare indeed.

However, one such occasion did occur on 23rd December 1889 when Stoke played Burnley at home. It was a fierce contest with Stoke winning 2-1 and Burnley claiming they had been intimidated. Yet Bob McCormick the Stoke inside-right, damaged his breast-bone in a strong challenge from a Burnley defender. Finally, the Stoke crowd invaded the pitch. Burnley protested to the League, demanding and winning a replay. Burnley won the replayed match 4-3.

On 23rd April 1910, Stoke and Port Vale's reserve sides met at the Victoria Ground to decide the North Staffordshire League championship. Former Stoke goalkeeper Dickie Roose was in the Vale side, and in fine form as his side led 2-0. The Stoke crowd gave vent to their anger and carried him off towards the River Trent. Fortunately for Roose, the police and the Stoke directors and club officials saved him from a ducking. Later the Welsh international goalkeeper claimed that he did not know the title was at stake, believing the match to be a friendly!

At the start of the 1977-78 season, the club's first game in the

Second Division, at Mansfield, saw them lose 2-1. City's fans let them down badly before, during and after the game. In the 1961-62 FA Cup fourth round tie against Blackburn Rovers, a controversial penalty was awarded which Bryan Douglas converted to take Rovers through to round five. The whole Stoke contingent took it badly and, indeed, one supporter started legal proceedings against the referee!

On 29th February, 1992, the League game with Birmingham City at St Andrew's was marred by a pitch invasion after Paul Barnes, the Stoke substitute, had equalised with just seconds left to play. Referee Roger Wiseman took the players off the field 'for their own protection'. After the St Andrew's ground had been emptied, the players returned and played the final 60 seconds at a walking pace!

D

DARWEN

They joined the League when it was extended to 14 clubs in 1891-92, but finished bottom of the table and conceded 112 goals in 26 games. That season, however, Darwen beat Stoke 9-3! The Potters did gain some revenge by winning their home fixture 5-1.

The two clubs met again in 1893-94 when each team won its home match 3-1. Darwen stayed in the Second Division until 1898-99 when they finished bottom of the table and conceded a League record 141 goals. They failed to gain re-election.

DAVIES, HARRY

The son of Harry Davies, the Wolves and Gainsborough Trinity full-back, he signed for Stoke from Bamfords Athletic in August 1922. He made his League debut at West Bromwich Albion on 23rd September, 1922, and in the return match, a week later, scored the only goal of the game. He twice played for Staffordshire against the Football League, but in April 1929 he was rather surprisingly sold to Huddersfield Town.

A replacement for the legendary Clem Stephenson, he appeared at

Wembley for the Terriers in their unsuccessful bid for the FA Cup of 1930. He was twice selected for an FA touring party for South Africa.

In February 1932, Stoke boss Tom Mather brought him back to the Victoria Ground, where he was to stay for a further six seasons. A scheming inside-forward, his delicate footwork helped the Potters to the Second Division title in 1933. After 410 League and Cup appearances for the club, in which he scored 101 goals, he was allowed to go to Port Vale in exchange for Tom Ward.

DEATH

John Proctor was a fine young player for Fenton and Dresden United before joining Stoke in August 1891. Following his debut in the 5-1 home win over Darwen on 5th December that year, he became a regular and was an ever-present the following season. Tragically, after just ten games of the 1893-94 season he became ill and died of pneumonia.

Reg Hodgkins joined Stoke from the Birmingham League side Hinckley United in September 1925, and though he made only 5 appearances in his two seasons, he was looked upon as a player for the future. In the summer of 1927 he was admitted to hospital in Coventry for an appendix operation, but died three weeks later.

Although he made only a few first team appearances, Paul Shardlow was extremely popular with the fans. He did keep goal for the club in the US Soccer Tourney, when they played as Cleveland Stokers, and acquitted himself with distinction. On 14th October 1968, the club went into mourning as he tragically collapsed and died at training. He had suffered a heart attack at the age of 25.

DEBUTS

Only two players have scored a hat-trick on their debuts for the club. They are Tom Hyslop, in a 4-1 win over Derby County on 23rd March 1895, and George Paterson, as Stoke beat Middlesbrough 4-0 on 26th September 1925.

A number of players have scored two goals on their debut for the club, the most recent being John Tudor on 18th September 1976. In fact, his first goal was very quick and has to rank in the dream category as the game's highlights were screened on BBC TV.

Brendan O'Callaghan had the distinction of scoring for Stoke with his first touch of the ball after coming on as substitute against Hull City on 8th March 1978 – it was the only goal of the game.

DEFEATS

Individual Games

Stoke's worst home defeat in a first-class match was the 6-1 result inflicted on the club by Tottenham Hotspur on 15th September 1951. Away from home, the club's heaviest defeat was the 10-0 thrashing inflicted by Preston North End on 14th September 1889.

Over a Single Season

Stoke's worst defensive record in terms of defeats suffered in a single season was in 1984-85 when the club lost 31 out of 42 First Division matches and were relegated. Conversely, the Potters lost only six matches from a 42 match programme in 1926-27 when they won the Third Division (North) Championship. They lost the same number in 1978-79 when they won promotion from Division Two.

Consecutive League Matches without defeat

Stoke's best run of League games without defeat is 25 and was established in 1992-93 as the club won the Second Division championship with 93 points. The run began on 5th September 1992 when the Potters drew 0-0 at home to Bolton Wanderers. They lost 1-0 to Leyton Orient on 27th February 1993. During the run they won 17 and drew eight games.

DEFENSIVE RECORDS

Stoke's best defensive record in the Football League was established in 1978-79; the club conceded just 31 goals to finish third in the Second Division and gain promotion. The club's worst defensive record in the Football League was in 1984-85 when they let in 91 goals in 42 matches. They finished bottom of the First Division and were relegated.

DISASTER

A terrible tragedy occurred at Burnden Park, the home of Bolton Wanderers, on 9th March 1946. Spectators were arriving for a sixth round FA Cup tie between Bolton and Stoke City. It was the second leg, the ties of the first post-war Cup being played on a home and away basis. Bolton had won the first-leg 2-0.

A huge crowd passed through the turnstiles to see, among others, Stoke's Stanley Matthews. The gates were closed with some 65,000 having paid, but another 20,000 were milling around outside and many managed to force their way in. Suddenly, two crash barriers

Burnden Park, 9 March 1946, scene of the Bolton Wanderers v Stoke City FA Cup sixth round tie in which 33 spectators lost their lives.

collapsed under the pressure. The result was horrific. Spectators piled on top of each other and many were trodden underfoot.

The match kicked off as casualties were being attended to, but as soon as it was known that there were fatalities, the referee called the players off the pitch. The police recommended the resumption of play to avoid panic as most of the crowd were unaware of the disaster. The match continued without any interval or any score. The death lists totalled 33 and more than 500 spectators were injured.

See also: Holditch Colliery

DISMISSALS

Although dismissals are a common feature of the modern game, no-one should think that football has ever been immune from them. The first Stoke player to be sent off in a Football League match was Ted Evans. He received his marching orders in the away game at Everton on 12th November 1892. Stoke drew 2-2.

John Ritchie came on to replace Alan Bloor in the second leg of the European Cup-Winners' Cup match against Kaiserslautern and was immediately sent off for striking an opponent who appeared to have spat at him.

England's 1966 World Cup hero Geoff Hurst was sent off for the first time in his career on 17th September 1972 while playing for Stoke City against Ipswich Town.

Peter Fox, the City goalkeeper, was sent off for handling the ball outside his penalty area against Luton Town on 25th September 1982. Disillusioned, he thought of quitting the game, but decided to carry on after many letters from well-wishers. The following month the FA decided that deliberate hand-ball was no longer considered as serious foul play.

DOBING, PETER

Coming from a sporting family (his father was a Rugby League player), Peter Dobing joined Blackburn Rovers where he won an FA Cup runners-up medal in 1959-60. After 179 League appearances for the Ewood Park club, he moved to Manchester City. He won 7 England

Under-23 caps and represented the Football League before his £37,500 transfer to Stoke in 1963.

Signed by Tony Waddington to strengthen a Stoke side that had just won promotion to the First Division, he went on to make 372 first team appearances in ten seasons at the Victoria Ground.

Undoubtedly his proudest day was when he led Stoke to victory in the 1972 Football League Cup Final. He came very close to winning full international honours, but lacked consistency. A broken leg at Ipswich on 17th October 1970 effectively ended his career, though it was 24th April 1973 before he played his last game for the Potters.

Peter Dobing: Captain of the Potters when they won the Football League Cup in 1972.

A keen cricketer, he came on as 12th man for Lancashire in a Roses match.

DODD, ALAN

One of the best central defenders in the club's post-war history, he emerged in the 1970s and had to compete initially with Stoke's formidable central pairing of Denis Smith and Alan Bloor.

He was skilful in the air and on the ground, and was highly regarded by Stoke manager Tony Waddington. He was the perfect example of consistency, making 102 consecutive League appearances from 10th January 1976 to 29th April 1978. The following season he was voted Player of the Year. However, there were occasions when his concentration seemed to lapse and this probably accounts for his failure to win full England honours when he seemed to be on the verge of adding to his six Under-23 caps.

Alan Durban and Richie Barker were less impressed by 'Doddy' and he was moved into midfield or played at full-back. He was eventually sold to Wolverhampton Wanderers in November 1982 for £40,000, and helped them win promotion in his first season.

In January 1985, Bill Asprey, desperately short of money, again signed him for Stoke, initially on a monthly contract. Unfortunately, he had lost his pace and was cruelly exposed by a number of top flight players as the club were relegated. He was granted a testimonial during the 1981-82 season and had a game against Port Vale at the Victoria Ground which the Potters won 3-2. A player who loved his football, he later had spells at Elfsborg, GAIS Gothenburg, Elfsborg (again), Port Vale, Cork City, Landskrona

Alan Dodd: One of the best central defenders never to win England recognition.

Bols, Rocester, Goldenhill Wanderers and Rocester again as player-coach.

DRAWS

Stoke played their greatest number of drawn League matches in a single season (19) in 1989-90 when they finished bottom of Division Two. In 1895-96 they went through the entire 30 match campaign without a draw, winning 15 and losing 15 matches to finish sixth in the First Division.

The club's highest scoring draw is 4-4, a score-line in six City matches: Bolton Wanderers (away 1892-93); Charlton Athletic (away 1929-30); Cardiff City (away 1959-60); Burnley (home 1963-64); Sheffield Wednesday (home 1963-64) and Luton Town (home 1982-83).

The greatest number of drawn matches in a single Stoke City FA Cup tie is four. This happened in 1954-55 when the Potters played Bury.

DURBAN, ALAN

Alan Durban was one of the players whose careers blossomed following the arrival of Brian Clough as manager at the Baseball Ground.
Under Clough he won a Second Division championship medal in
1968-69 and a League Championship medal in 1971-72. Though he
scored 112 goals in his 403 appearances for the Rams, he developed
more into a constructive midfield player.

He became manager of Shrewsbury in February 1974 and steered
the club out of the Fourth Division in 1974-75, and later into the
Second Division and to Welsh Cup success.

Appointed manager of Stoke in February 1978, he began to introduce more discipline into the club. With Howard Kendall promoted
to player-coach, Stoke won promotion to Division One in 1978-79.
Although Durban made a number of signings in the summer, the club
struggled to avoid relegation the following season.

Durban's ambitions were bigger than Stoke City's, and in the
summer of 1981 he was tempted by Sunderland's offer and became
their manager. He had commanded great respect from the Stoke
faithful, but many of them were very bitter at some of his parting
comments. He pleaded the case of Richie Barker, his former assistant
at Shrewsbury and then assistant at Wolves, and the board duly
appointed Barker in succession.

After three years at Roker Park, Durban was sacked. He later
managed Cardiff City, but is now assistant-manager of his former
club, Derby County.

Stoke City's full League record under Alan Durban was:

P.	W.	D.	L.	F.	A.
142	53	47	42	180	169

DURHAM CITY

Durham City spent seven seasons in the Football League, from 1921
to 1928 when they were not re-elected. They were always in the Third
Division (North). The two clubs met in the 1926-27 season when
Stoke won 4-0 at home and 2-1 away to complete the double.

E

EARLY GROUNDS

The exact location of Stoke's original playing pitches is almost as much a mystery as the club's own origins. The original pitch was situated on what is the present burial ground in Lonsdale Street, although they also played on pitches near to the Copeland Arms and in Campbell Road.

George Eastham: Scorer of the second goal in Stoke's 2-1 League Cup Final win over Chelsea in 1972.

EASTHAM, GEORGE

When he played for England against Brazil at Wembley in May 1963, it was the first time that a father and son had gained caps for their country. He had played alongside his father at Ards in Ulster before signing for Newcastle United. When the Magpies refused to transfer list him after he had asked for a move, he went on strike and won a famous High Court case, in the process helping to change the 'retain and transfer' system in British football. From Newcastle United he moved to Arsenal where he built on his reputation, winning in total 19 full caps to add to his 6 Under-23 caps and 3 Football League appearances.

He was a member of England's 1966 World Cup squad, but did not play.

In August 1966 he signed for Stoke for £35,000. He appeared in the club's first Wembley Cup Final, scoring the second goal as they beat Chelsea 2-1 in March 1972.

He then started to develop his coaching ambitions and went to South Africa with Cape Town Spurs and then Hellenic as player-manager. He rejoined Stoke as assistant to Tony Waddington, taking over as manager on Waddington's dismissal. He had little money to spend and the stars that were still at the Victoria Ground wanted to get away. He was sacked after a 3-2 defeat at the hands of non-League Blyth Spartans in the FA Cup in February 1978.

Stoke City's full League record under George Eastham was:

P.	W.	D.	L.	F.	A.
38	9	12	17	37	52

ELECTION

Following their success in winning the Second Division of the Southern League, Stoke sought election to the Football League at the Annual General Meeting held on 19th July 1915. The two bottom clubs, Leicester Fosse and Glossop, had to seek re-election and as Stoke secured 21 votes to Glossop's one, they were elected. Later in the meeting, however, the League confirmed that only regional football would be played in the next season.

EVER-PRESENTS

There have been 63 Stoke City players who have been ever-present throughout a Football League season. The greatest number of ever-present seasons by a City player is three, the record being held by Tom Clare, Bob McGrory, Arthur Turner and Bill Asprey.

The full list is:

Number of Seasons   **Players**

3   B. Asprey, T. Clare, B. McGrory, A. Turner.

2   T. Allen. G. Baddeley, F. Bowyer, D. Brodie, H. Burrows, W. Dickson, A. Dodd, P. Fox, N. Gleghorn, T. Holford, J. McCue, E. Skeels, F. Soo, A. Underwood.

1   R. Archibald, A. Beachill, K. Bertschin, W. Biggins, W. Bourne, P. Bracewell, J. Bradley, D. Christie, A. Clark, G. Clarke, G. Clawley, N. Coleman, G. Crooks, L. Dixon, A. Ford, A. Hudson, F. Johnson, T. Kay, H. Kendall, J. King, W. McReddie, R. McSkimming, A. Milne, F. Mountford, J. Murphy, J. O'Neill, M. Pejic, J. Proctor, B. Ralphs, R. Ramsey, D. Ratcliffe, T. Robertson, W. Robertson, W. Rowley, J. Salmons, L. Sandford, C. Scrimshaw, H. Sellars, J. Sellars, P. Shilton, L. Sigurdsson, W. Spencer, W. Turner, A. Tutin, A. Urmston.

F

FATHER AND SON

Between the mid 20s and the late 50s, Harry Sellars and his son John made an enormous contribution to the cause of Stoke City Football Club. Making his debut on 26th January 1924, Harry Sellars made 394 League and Cup appearances, scoring 21 goals. John Sellars played in 413 games, scoring 15 goals, after making his first team debut on 1st February 1946.

FESTIVAL OF BRITAIN

In 1951, the Potters played two games in the Festival of Britain, beating Schiedam VC 2-1 and Oporto 2-0.

FEWEST DEFEATS

The fewest defeats suffered by Stoke City over a full League season was six in seasons 1926-27 and 1978-79.

In 1926-27, the club won the Third Division (North) championship and yet lost to New Brighton 5-0, Rochdale 4-0 and Bradford Park Avenue 3-0. In 1978-79, the club won promotion to the First Division.

FEWEST GOALS

Stoke City scored just 24 goals in 42 Division One matches in 1984-85. They did not score more than two goals in any one game and failed to score at all in 25. With 17 points, they were 23 behind their nearest rivals Sunderland, and were relegated in last place.

FEWEST WINS

Stoke achieved only three wins in 22 Division One matches in 1889-90. They finished bottom with 10 points, only one fewer than the previous season when they had won just four games. They failed to gain re-election, but subsequently returned to the League in 1891 when it was extended to 14 clubs.

They also achieved only three wins in 42 matches in the First Division in 1984-85. Their 17 points included just eight from drawn games and ensured relegation. The club also set records for most defeats, fewest goals scored and fewest points in a season in the division.

FIRST DIVISION

Stoke's first match, on 8th September 1888, saw them lose 2-0 at home to West Bromwich Albion. At the end of their first season they finished bottom of the League, albeit on goal average. They failed to improve the following season and again finished at the foot of the table. However, this time they failed to gain re-election and Sunderland took their place.

For 1891-92 the Football League was increased from 12 to 14 clubs and Stoke were able to rejoin after collecting more votes than Derby County and West Bromwich Albion, two of the existing teams. There were a number of occasions in those early years when the club was faced with Second Division football, and at the end of the 1906-07 season they were finally relegated. The club's best position in that spell was sixth in 1902-03.

Promoted in 1921-22, the club's second spell in the top flight lasted just one season as they found themselves stranded at the foot of the table almost immediately – drawing two and losing six of their opening eight matches. The club continued to struggle, and even spent one season in the Third Division (North) before returning to the First Division at the end of the 1932-33 season.

In 1935-36, Bob McGrory's first season in charge, Stoke finished fourth, the highest position in the club's history. In 1946-47 the club equalled that feat, and almost won the League. Needing to win at Bramall Lane, Stoke lost 2-1 to Sheffield United, thus handing the title to Liverpool. There followed six seasons of struggling before the club were relegated.

Winning promotion in 1962-63, the club had a number of years of mid-table placings before finishing fifth in seasons 1973-74 and 1974-75. In this latter season, the club had a great chance of winning the League Championship with three games remaining to be played. However, they lost at Sheffield United (again!) and drew with New-castle United and Burnley. As it transpired, they would have won the title if they'd won all three games!

Relegated in 1976-77, the Potters were back in Division One in 1979-80, but within six seasons returned to the Second Division after a disastrous 1984-85 campaign.

Following the reorganisation of the Football League and the intro-duction of the Premier League, the club found themselves back in the First Division for the 1993-94 season. In the 1995-96 season the club reached the play-offs, but went down to a Garry Parker goal in the second leg at the Victoria Ground after the first leg at Filbert Street had been goalless.

Stoke's record in the First Division is:

P.	W.	D.	L.	F.	A.
2130	714	515	911	2818	3293

FIRST LEAGUE MATCH

Stoke's first League game was on 8th September 1888, at home to West Bromwich Albion. The attendance was reported as 4,524 and the Stoke side was as follows: Rowley, Clare, Underwood, Ramsey, Shutt, Smith, Sayer, McSkimming, Staton, Edge and Tunnicliffe. Albion were in command virtually throughout the game, yet their first goal was a long time in coming. They rained shots in at the Stoke goal for most of the first-half, and Stoke 'keeper Rowley did extremely well to save everything. The Potters threatened only occasionally, but big Ben Roberts in the Albion goal had to be at his international best to prevent shots from Staton and Tunnicliffe crossing the line. At half-time there was still no score. The long awaited breakthrough for Albion came with only six minutes remaining. Rowley, under pres-sure, threw the ball hurriedly, straight to the feet of Albion's Joe Wilson who quickly fired it back over the stranded 'keeper. In the last minute, Billy Bassett got away down the right wing and from his measured cross, George Woodhall headed a second goal to clinch victory for Albion.

FIRST MATCHES

The first game that the club played was on 17th October 1868 when, as Stoke Ramblers, they played Mr E.W. May's Fifteen and drew 1-1.

Henry Almond captained the Ramblers and scored the goal. The club's first match against other opposition was at Congleton – a rugby team! On a heavy pitch, Stoke's advantage was cancelled out and the game also ended in a 1-1 draw.

Stoke's 1-0 win over Port Vale in the FA Cup qualifying round on 5th October 1887 was the club's first game in what we would now describe as a first-class competition.

FLOODLIGHTS

Stoke's first game under floodlights was on 27th February 1890 when they defeated Crewe Alexandra 3-1 under Wells Lights.

Europe's first set of permanent floodlights had been erected at the Olympic Stadium in Amsterdam in 1934, and were first switched on for a game between an Amsterdam XI and Stoke City.

After floodlights were installed at the Victoria Ground in the 1956-57 season, the club's first game under them was against Port Vale when 38,729 saw City win 3-1. The floodlighting system gave Stoke the opportunity to bring foreign opposition to play at the Victoria Ground and the first two were Radnicki from Yugoslavia, who were beaten 3-0, and Essen from West Germany, who were defeated 5-0.

When the Stoke End Stand was opened in October 1979, its erection dictated a change of the floodlighting system since the original pylons had stood on the open banking. In their place were installed two smaller, more compact pylons and so the Victoria Ground had two different pairs of lights.

FOOD POISONING

On 4th January 1902, Stoke's pre-match meal at Liverpool was one of plaice, but the players contracted food poisoning and the side was reduced to seven men in the second half through illness. They lost 7-0, and also lost their next seven games!

FOOTBALL ALLIANCE

Following their failure to gain re-election at the end of the 1889-90 season, Stoke joined the Football Alliance which operated a 12 team league and was very much the secondary competition to the Football League. It was made up of teams from the North and the Midlands. Stoke found life in this competition much easier and finished the season as Champions, three points clear of their nearest rivals, Sunderland Albion. It was the club's only season in the Alliance as the following year the Football League decided to increase the size of the League from 12 to 14 clubs and Stoke rejoined. The club's record that season was:

P.	W.	D.	L.	F.	A.	Pts.
22	13	7	2	57	30	33

FOOTBALL ASSOCIATION CUP

Stoke first joined the competition in 1884-85 when it was more usually referred to as the English Cup. They withdrew from their first Qualifying Round game against Queen's Park in Glasgow, leaving the home side with a walkover. They fared little better the following season, losing 1-0 after extra-time in a replay at Crewe Alexandra after the first match at Stoke had been drawn 2-2. The club's first FA Cup win came on 30th October 1886 when Caernarfon Wanderers were beaten 10-1. In 1887-88 Stoke reached the First Round proper after Qualifying Round wins over Port Vale, Wanderers and Oswestry, plus a bye. Unfortunately, they then lost 4-1 at West Bromwich Albion.

In 1898-99, Stoke reached the semi-final of the FA Cup for the first time after accounting for Sheffield Wednesday, Birmingham and Tottenham Hotspur. They then lost 3-1 to Derby County at Molineux, with Steve Bloomer scoring a hat-trick for the Rams.

In 1926-27, the season the Potters won the Third Division (North) championship, they surprisingly lost to Rhyl Athletic from the Welsh League in a second replay at Old Trafford.

After winning promotion to the top flight in 1932-33, City reached the quarter-final of the competition the following season, only to be drawn away to Manchester City. The Potters took an amazing following with them to Maine Road and so swelled the attendance to 84,569 – a record crowd for a club game in England outside Wembley!

The next time City reached the semi-final stage was in 1970-71 when, after beating Millwall, Huddersfield Town, Ipswich and Hull, Stoke lost 2-0 to Arsenal in a replay at Villa Park.

There were similarities the following year when another semi-final tie with Arsenal was achieved, this time following victories over Chesterfield, Tranmere Rovers, Hull City and Manchester United. Again the semi-final went to a replay and a 2-1 reverse at Goodison Park.

The club's best performance in recent years was in 1986-87 when they reached the fifth round, only to lose 1-0 at home to Coventry City, the eventual winners of the trophy.

Stoke's full record in the FA Cup is:

P.	W.	D.	L.	F.	A.
289	105	81	103	448	401

FOOTBALLER OF THE YEAR

Two Stoke City players have been honoured by the Football Writers' Association as their choice for Footballer of the Year.

1963	Stanley Matthews
1972	Gordon Banks

FOOTBALL LEAGUE CUP

Sad to relate, in recent years the Potters have failed to make much impact upon the Football League (later Milk, Littlewoods, Rumblelows and Coca Cola) Cup.

In fact, Stoke made very little impact in the first three seasons, losing to Doncaster Rovers, Charlton Athletic and then beaten finalists Aston Villa in the first three competitions. However, in 1963-64 John Ritchie scored 10 goals as Stoke reached the final against Leicester City. It was a two-legged affair – a 1-1 draw at the Victoria Ground was insufficient and Leicester took the Cup with a 3-2 win in the return at Filbert Street.

It was the 1971-72 tournament that was to see the club's finest hour.

After beating Southport and Oxford United, Stoke visited Old Trafford in the fourth round and drew 1-1 in front of a 47,062 crowd. The replay attracted 40,829 fans to the Victoria Ground, but there were no goals and a third game was required.

This was again played at Stoke and 42,233 turned up to see Dobing and Ritchie score for City in a 2-1 win. Eight days later, a 4-2 win at Bristol Rovers saw Stoke enter the League Cup semi-final, where they met West Ham United over two legs. The epic tie was finally settled in the second play-off at Old Trafford. West Ham won the first leg at Stoke 2-1, but Stoke equalised at Upton Park and then took the tie into extra-time. With three minutes left, Gordon Banks made a brilliant penalty save from World Cup colleague Geoff Hurst. The first play-off, at Hillsborough, was goalless, and so the fourth and ultimately deciding game took place on 26th January 1972. There was early drama as West Ham's goalkeeper, Ferguson, had gone off injured. Bobby Moore went in goal and saved Mike Bernard's penalty, though he followed up to score. West Ham, with ten men, then took the game to Stoke and took the lead with goals by Bonds and Brooking. When Ferguson returned, Stoke seemed to play better against the full side and Dobing equalised. Within minutes of the resumption of play in the second half, Conroy put Stoke in front again. The Hammers came storming back, but had to admit defeat after 420 minutes of football. On their first ever visit to Wembley, the Stoke side was: Banks, Marsh, Pejic, Bernard, Smith, Bloor, Conroy, Greenhoff, Ritchie, Dobing and Eastham, with Mahoney substitute.

George Eastham at 35 and Gordon Banks at 34 had a big say in Stoke's 2-1 triumph over Chelsea. Eastham scored the winner, his first goal in 18 months, and Banks made two late saves that demonstrated why he was considered one of the world's greatest goalkeepers. Credit was also due to Terry Conroy whose brave one-man raids kept Stoke in the game when Chelsea were threatening to crush them. He scored the first goal, a header, after five minutes and made the cross that led to Stoke's winning goal.

The club's best score-line was established when City beat Chelsea (again!) 6-2 on 22nd October 1974.

John Ritchie holds the record number of appearances in the competition for the club, with a total of 38. He also heads the goal-scoring chart with a total of 18.

Stoke City's record to date in the League Cup (correct to June 1996) is as follows:

P.	W.	D.	L.	F.	A.
120	49	31	40	160	152

FORMATION

It had always been assumed that Stoke's origins dated as far back as 1863, but fairly recent research by Wade Martin, the club's historian, put the formation in 1868. A couple of Old Carthusians, apprentices at the North Staffordshire Railway Company, formed Stoke Ramblers with some of their workmates. Forty years later, Stoke went bankrupt and a new club was formed.

FORMER CLUBS

Centre-forward Andy Graver, known as 'The Homing Pigeon', had the experience, while playing for Stoke City, of playing against one or other of his former clubs on four successive Saturdays in 1956.

v Leicester City	Away	FA Cup	on 28th January
v Lincoln City	Away	League	on 4th February
v Leicester City	Home	League	on 11th February
v Newcastle United	Away	FA Cup	on 18th February

FOREIGN PLAYERS

During the 1965-66 season, Stoke manager Tony Waddington tried to sign Swedish international Sven Larrson and, indeed, played him in a home friendly match against Moscow Dynamo. Permission was denied, however, and the club were fined 100 guineas.

Stoke's first foreign import was Loek Ursem who was signed for £85,000 from AZ67 Alkmaar. Though he never commanded a regular place in the side and lacked a little pace, the Dutch Under-21 international was popular with the Stoke faithful.

In the summer of 1993, manager Lou Macari signed Icelandic international Toddy Orlygsson on a free transfer from Nottingham Forest. He appeared in 90 League games for the Potters before joining Oldham Athletic. His cousin, Larus Sigurdsson, joined the club and

Peter Fox: holder of the club record for the most appearances for a goalkeeper.

was an ever-present in the 1995-96 season. Canadian-born Paul Peschisolido joined the club from Birmingham City and was later to rejoin the St Andrew's club.

City have also loaned three foreign goalkeepers – Hans Segers (Nottingham Forest); Jason Kearton (Everton) and Bruce Grobbelaar (Liverpool).

The club have also had on their books some players who, though not born on foreign shores, had very foreign-sounding names – notably George Antonio, Lucien Boullimier, Louie Donowa, Mel Pejic and John Ruggiero.

FOX, PETER

He started his career at Sheffield Wednesday, and is still the youngest player ever to appear for the Owls' first team – at 15 years 8 months He made 49 appearances for the Hillsborough club before loan spells at West Ham, Barnsley and with Team Hawaii in the NASL. In March 1978, Stoke boss Alan Durban paid £15,000 to bring him to the Victoria Ground.

Initially, he was deputy to Roger Jones, but soon won a first team place, making his debut in a 3-0 home win over Wrexham in December 1978. 'Foxy' turned out to be the Potters' number one for over a dozen seasons, and with 477 appearances to his name, he holds the club record for a goalkeeper. During his time at Stoke a number of back injuries interrupted his career, otherwise he would have made even more starts.

Extremely popular with the Stoke fans, he earned a testimonial game for his loyal service. Other keepers were signed who appeared to threaten his position, but in 1992-93, despite a number of loan signings, it was 'Foxy' who won a medal in the club's Autoglass Trophy success at Wembley. The following season, Lou Macari turned to 'Foxy' in the vital run to win the Second Division championship.

Following a spell on loan at Linfield, he became player-coach to Alan Ball at Exeter City in July 1993, and became the Grecians' manager in June 1995.

FRANKLIN, NEIL

In the history of the game there has probably not been a more accomplished footballer in an England defence than Neil Franklin.

After the end of the Second World War, he was the unchallenged England centre-half for 27 consecutive matches. He had gained 10 war-time caps as the successor to the legendary Stan Cullis, but his career was disrupted by a secret and ill-advised departure from Stoke City for the Sante Fe club of Bogota, Colombia.

Together with George Mountford, Stoke's outside-right, Franklin and his family left for South America in the spring of 1950, having signed contracts immediately after the end of the domestic season. He told the Football Association that he would not be available for the World Cup finals in Brazil because his wife was expecting their second child and she planned to have the baby in Bogota.

Neil Franklin: An accomplished defender whose career was disrupted by his decision to go to Columbia.

This was the era of the maximum wage of £20-a-week in English football, and there was no freedom of contract once a player had signed for a club. In spite of McGrory's dislike of Franklin's stylish, intelligent game, Stoke had refused Franklin's request for a move.

In the event, his wife decided to fly home for the birth. The Stoke defender accompanied her as far as New York, as had been agreed, but then, on finding no flight booked for his wife, flew back with her to England. For breach of contract at the Victoria Ground Franklin was suspended without pay until the following year. An illustrious career had been destroyed.

He subsequently joined Hull City for £22,500, but was never again selected for England. A crowd of 55,000 greeted Franklin's first appearance for the Tigers, but a later cartilage injury curtailed his success. After brief moves to Crewe, Stockport and Macclesfield, he became a player-manager with Wellington, then manager of Colchester in the Football League, leading them to promotion to the Third Division in 1966.

FRIENDLIES

Stoke City have played host to a number of opponents in friendly matches. Below is a full list of City's home matches in this category when foreign opposition visited the Victoria Ground.

Season:	Opponents:	Result:	Score:
1934-35	F.C. Austria	Won	1-0
1935-36	Slavia Prague	Won	2-1
1938-39	Racing Club de Paris	Lost	0-1
1950-51	Schiedam V.C.	Won	2-1
1950-51	Oporto	Won	2-0
1956-57	Radnicki	Won	3-1
1957-58	Olympique Nice	Won	6-1
1957-58	Singen	Won	5-1
1957-58	Stuttgart K.	Won	3-2
1958-59	First Vienna	Drew	1-1
1962-63	Real Madrid	Drew	2-2
1963-64	Benfica	Lost	0-1
1965-66	Moscow Dynamo	Lost	0-2
1969-70	Asante Kotoko	Won	3-2
1969-70	Santos	Lost	2-3
1969-70	Dallas Tornados	Won	6-1
1979-80	NEC Nijmegen	Won	4-1
1993-94	Real Sociedad	Won	2-0
1994-95	FC Xanthi	Lost	2-3

FULL MEMBERS' CUP

Originally called the Full Members' Cup because it was open only to First and Second Division clubs, Stoke's first match in the competition saw them defeat Coventry City 3-0 in front of a Victoria Ground crowd of 3,516. Following a 2-2 draw at Millwall, where Keith Bertschin again scored from the penalty spot, the Potters then played at home to Oxford United. Despite a great deal of pressure, Stoke couldn't break down the visitors' defence and Oxford won 1-0.

G

GAINSBOROUGH TRINITY

They spent sixteen seasons in the Second Division between 1896 and 1912, and never managed to finish any higher than sixth. The two clubs met five times, all in the 1907-08 season. Their first encounter, on 5th October 1907, saw Stoke win 5-0, with goals from Holford (2), Fielding, Gemmell and Watkins. However, Trinity won the return match 2-0. The sides were also drawn together that season in the second round of the FA Cup and it took Stoke three attempts before they won 3-2 at Nottingham.

GLOSSOP NORTH END

They won promotion to the First Division at the end of their first season in the League, 1898-99. They were relegated the following season and spent the rest of the time in the lower division. They finished bottom of the table in the last season before World War One, 1914-15, and resigned from the League shortly before the resumption of matches in 1919. Stoke met Glossop in the 1899-1900 season only. After drawing 1-1 at home, they won 2-1 away with both goals being scored by Joe Turner.

GOALKEEPERS

Stoke City FC has almost always been extremely well served by its goalkeepers, and most of them have been extremely popular with the supporters. Many names spring to mind, such as Bill Rowley, Jack Robinson, Leigh Richmond Roose, Dennis Herod, Gordon Banks, Peter Shilton and Peter Fox.

Bill Rowley was Stoke's first goalkeeper in the Football League, and their first international goalkeeper. There are a number of stories associated with this man. Having started his career as a centre-forward with Hanley Orion, he first joined Stoke in 1883, but stayed only a year before joining Burslem Port Vale. In the final of the Burslem Challenge Cup, Vale demolished Ironbridge 12-0. Bill was so bored that he joined in the attack, and even scored one of the goals!

Jack Robinson was 43 when he signed for Stoke, and thus became one of the oldest players to make his first appearance for the club.

Dr Leigh Richmond Roose was one of the most famous amateur goalkeepers of the pre-World War One period. As an amateur, he played for a variety of clubs and, in fact, signed for different sides at different times for different leagues. A wealthy man, he once hired his own train to get him to an Aston Villa match!

On one occasion, Port Vale visited the Victoria Ground for a game against Stoke Reserves that would decide the North Staffordshire and District League championship. Roose was one of four notable amateurs signed for this game. With Vale leading 2-0, the Stoke supporters stormed the pitch and carried Roose towards the River Trent for a ducking. The Stoke Chairman, Revd. A.E. Hurst, ran on to the pitch to appeal for calm, and Stoke forward Horrocks was knocked unconscious before Roose was released with the help of the police.

On 16th February 1952, Dennis Herod became the only goalkeeper to date to score for Stoke in a first-class game. He was injured at Villa Park and so played out on the wing to try to cause the Villa defence as much trouble as possible. However, he popped up to score Stoke's third goal in a 3-2 win.

Arguably, of course, Gordon Banks is the greatest goalkeeper of all time. In the 1970 World Cup in Mexico, while a Stoke player, he made the famous save from a header from the legendary Pele. Pele is reported to have shouted 'goal' as soon as he headed the ball. A most likeable man, his consistency was legendary and his contribution at Wembley in 1972, when Stoke won the League Cup, was immense.

One of the greatest goalkeepers in the modern era was Peter Shilton. Tony Waddington paid Leicester City £325,000 to secure Shilton for a World record fee for a keeper, yet Stoke fans never really saw him at his best.

Always popular with Stoke fans, Peter Fox spent 15 years at the club and broke the record number of appearances for a goalkeeper.

GOAL-SCORING

For the club:

Stoke's highest goal-scoring tally was achieved in 1926-27 when the team that won the Third Division (North) championship hit 92 League goals in 42 matches.

By the individual:

The following players have scored 50 or more League goals for the club:

Freddie Steele	1934-1949	140
Frank Bowyer	1948-1960	137
John Ritchie	1963-1966 and 1969-1974	135
Charlie Wilson	1926-1931	110
Johnny King	1953-1961	106
Harry Oscroft	1950-1959	103
Tommy Sale	1930-1936 and 1938-1939	98
Harry Davies	1922-1929 and 1932-1937	92
Joe Schofield	1891-1899	84
Peter Dobing	1963-1972	82
Jimmy Greenhoff	1969-1976	76
Willie Maxwell	1895-1901	75
Harry Burrows	1965-1973	68
Alf Smith	1904 and 1910-1915	67
Arty Watkin	1913-1923 and 1924-1925	64
Jimmy Broad	1921-1924	62
Bobby Liddle	1928-1938	61
Dennis Viollet	1962-1967	59
Billy Smith	1909-1913	57
Joe Johnson	1932-1937	54
Stanley Matthews	1932-1947 and 1961-1965	54
Mark Stein	1991-1993	51
Wayne Biggins	1989-1992 and 1994-1995	50

All dates refer to calendar years of debuts and last appearances. Correct to June 1996.

GOAL-SCORING EXPLOITS

In 1957, Stoke's winger, Neville Coleman, scored seven goals in their Division Two match against Lincoln City, a record by a winger in the Football League.

Charlie Wilson holds the Stoke record for the most goals in a season. In 1927-28, he scored a total of 38 goals; 32 in the League and six in the FA Cup.

While Freddie Steele was the club's leading marksman in five successive peacetime seasons either side of World War Two, John Ritchie holds the club record. He was Stoke's top marksman seven times during his two spells at the Victoria Ground.

During the 1995-96 season, Mike Sheron rewrote a chapter of Stoke's 128-year history book with a record breaking seventh goal in successive games. The former Manchester City player struck spectacularly in the 29th minute of a ferocious assault on Charlton Athletic's goal at the Victoria Ground on 17th April, beating a record shared by John Ritchie in the 1960s and Charlie Wilson in the 1920s.

GREENHOFF, JIMMY

Jimmy Greenhoff was discovered by Leeds United after he played an important part in Barnsley Boys winning the English Schools Trophy

in 1961. He made 94 League appearances for the Elland Road club before Don Revie sold him to Birmingham City in the middle of an Inter Cities Fairs Cup Final against Ferencvaros. Greenhoff had played in the first leg.

After one season, and 31 appearances, for the St Andrew's club, he was signed by Tony Waddington in August 1969 for £100,000. Making his debut at Wolverhampton in the opening match of that season, he went on to make 338 League and Cup appearances for the Potters, scoring 97 goals. He formed an almost telepathic understanding with

Jimmy Greenhoff: Idolised by the Stoke fans, he scored 97 goals for the Potters in 338 League and Cup appearances.

Alan Hudson in midfield and a fine partnership up front with John Ritchie. He had already won a League Cup winners' medal with Leeds in 1968 and earned another in 1972 when he helped Stoke beat Chelsea.

In November 1976, the unthinkable happened – Jimmy Greenhoff joined Manchester United for £120,000. One of the most popular Stoke players of all time, he was idolised by the fans for his his skills and work rate. At Old Trafford he won an FA Cup winners' medal in 1977 and a runners-up medal in 1979.

After playing for United, he played for Crewe, Toronto Blizzards, Port Vale, Rochdale and Vale again as player-coach. He won five Under-23 caps and represented the Football League, yet, surprisingly, this most gifted of footballers did not win a full cap.

GUEST PLAYERS

The 'Guest' system was used by all the clubs during the two wars. Although at times it was abused almost beyond belief (some sides that opposed Stoke had ten or eleven 'guests'!), it normally worked sensibly and effectively to the benefit of the players, clubs and supporters.

Stoke's players frequently 'guested' elsewhere, and in May 1942, City's Freddie Steele and Harry Ware both played for the Northampton Town side that defeated Stoke 10-0 at the County Ground!

Stoke, too, had many 'guests' during both wars who were, or later became internationals. These included Sid Bower (West Bromwich Albion), Sammy Brooks (Wolverhampton Wanderers) and Harry Hampton (Aston Villa) in the First World War, and Newcastle's Tom Pearson in the Second World War. Other players who 'guested' for the Potters during the Second World War were Jack Griffiths, the Manchester United left-back; Charlton Athletic's John Oakes; Charlie Scrimshaw back from the north-east; and Lol Hamlett of Bolton Wanderers, who later became Port Vale's trainer for many years.

HALIFAX TOWN

The Shaymen lost their Football League status at the end of the 1992-93 season. Having played their first Football League game on

27th August 1921 in the Third Division (north), the club endured sixty-five seasons without winning a League Championship. The two clubs met only in the 1926-27 season, with the first encounter at the Shay ending 2-2. The return fixture was Stoke's last game of a season which saw them crowned as champions of the Third Division (North). The Potters won 5-1 with goals from Harry Davies (2), Johnny Eyres (2) and Bobby Archibald.

HAT-TRICKS

Stoke City players have netted 90 hat-tricks in Football League games. Freddie Steele holds the record with 12.

The last hat-trick hero in a League game for City was Simon Sturridge against Southend United on 11th November 1995. Stoke finally won 4-2.

Two Stoke players scored hat-tricks on their debuts for the club in Football League matches. Tom Hyslop scored a hat-trick on his debut against Derby County on 23rd March 1895 as Stoke won 4-1, whilst George Paterson hit his in a 4-0 win over Middlesbrough on 26th September 1925. Strangely, Paterson played only a further six games for the club. Another player to score a hat-trick on his debut for the club was George Lenaghan in a 4-3 win over West Ham United in a Southern League match on 16th December 1911.

There have been a number of occasions when two Stoke players have scored hat-tricks in the same match, but only one in the Football League. That occurred on 11th September 1937 when Steele (5) and Jim Westland (3) helped the Potters to an 8-1 win over Derby County. The only occasion when a player has scored a double hat-trick in the Football League came on 23rd February 1957 when Neville Coleman scored seven of the goals in City's 8-0 win over Lincoln. During the wartime games of the Second World War, Tommy Sale scored six in the club's 8-0 win over Walsall on 3rd January 1942, and Freddie Steele scored six in the 9-3 victory over Wolves on 1st January 1944.

Although 44 players have scored Football League hat-tricks for the club, it is surprising to find that Harry Oscroft, who scored 103 League goals for City, managed only one hat-trick.

Moreover, Harry Davies, who grabbed 92 League goals for Stoke, somehow failed to register a hat-trick for the club.

HODGE, PETER

Entering football administration with a local boys' club in his home town of Dunfermline, he was later involved with Dunfermline Juniors and Athletic before becoming manager of Raith Rovers. He took this club into the First Division.

In June 1914, Hodge was recruited by Stoke, then a Southern League Second Division club, as a replacement for Alfred Barker. After winning the championship of the Southern League Second Division, the club successfully re-applied to rejoin the Football League, but, of course, the League competition was abandoned because of the First World War.

During the war he returned to Scotland to manage Raith Rovers again. He returned to English football in 1919 as Leicester manager and saw them into the First Division before accepting an offer to become Manchester City's manager in 1926. In his first season in charge, City just missed promotion from the Second Division. In 1927-28 they were promoted as champions, and they finished third in the First Division the following season.

He later returned to Leicester, but was taken ill shortly after Portsmouth had beaten the Filberts in the 1934 FA Cup semi-final. He died less than 48 hours later.

HOLDITCH COLLIERY

The tragic loss of life at Holditch Colliery was marked with a 'Disaster Game'. The visitors were Scottish giants Glasgow Rangers and Stoke held them to a goalless draw in front of a large crowd.

HOLFORD, TOM

Having played for Granville's Night School and Cobridge, he joined Stoke in May 1898 on wages of £1 per week. A fine utility player who could play in a variety of positions, it took him three seasons to hold down a regular first-team spot.

Although the Hanley-born defender was never sent off, he was known as 'Dirty Tommy', an affectionate nickname for the way he played the game! An excellent passer of the ball, he won an England cap in 1903 when he was acclaimed as the smallest centre-half (he was 5ft 5ins) to play for England.

He stayed at the Victoria Ground until the club went bankrupt in 1908 when he signed for Manchester City. He scored three hat-tricks in the space of twenty-one days in 1909-10 when City won the Second Division championship.

In 1914 he joined Port Vale and spent 36 years with them as player, trainer and scout. In 1924, with the club desperate for players, he came out of retirement at the age of 46 – the oldest player to appear for Vale.

HOME MATCHES

Excluding the pre-Football League matches and City's spell in the Southern and Birmingham Leagues, the club's best home wins have been the 10-3 victory over West Bromwich Albion in a Division One match on 4th February 1937; the 9-0 victory over Plymouth Argyle in a Second Division encounter in December 1960; and the 9-1 win over Ipswich Town in the First Division on 21st March 1964.

The Potters have scored eight goals at home on three occasions:

Leeds United 8-1 in 1934-35; Derby County 8-1 in 1937-38 and Lincoln City 8-0 in 1956-57.

Stoke's worst home defeat was 6-1 against Tottenham Hotspur on 15th September 1951. They have also conceded five goals at home on four occasions: Middlesbrough 2-5 in 1955-56; Bristol Rovers 3-5 in 1957-58; Leeds United 1-5 in 1968-69 and Liverpool 1-5 in 1981-82.

The highest scoring home match, other than those mentioned, is City's 7-2 victory over Leeds United on 21st December 1986, though there have been three 4-4 draws: Burnley 1963-64; Sheffield Wednesday 1963-64 and Luton Town 1982-83.

HOME SEASONS

Though Stoke City have not gone through a complete League season with an undefeated home record, they have gone through a campaign suffering just one home defeat on five occasions:

	P.	W.	D.	L.	F.	A.
1893-94 Division 1	15	13	1	1	45	17
1921-22 Division 2	21	9	11	1	31	11
1923-24 Division 2	21	9	11	1	27	10
1926-27 Division 3 (N)	21	17	3	1	57	11
1931-32 Division 2	21	14	6	1	47	19

City's highest number of home wins in a League season is 17. They achieved this number of victories in both 1926-27 and 1992-93 when they were champions of Division Three (North) and Division Two respectively.

HONOURS

The major honours achieved by the club are:

Football League Cup Winners	1971-72
Football League Cup Runners-Up	1963-64
Second Division Champions	1932-33
	1962-63
	1992-93
Second Division Runners-Up	1921-22
Third Division (North) Champions	1926-27
Autoglass Trophy Winners	1991-92
FA Cup semi-finalists	1898-99
	1970-71
	1971-72

HUDSON, ALAN

One of the most gifted players of his generation, he signed for Stoke from Chelsea in January 1974 for £240,000. Known for his love of the bright lights of the King's Road, Chelsea, he soon settled in Stoke and for the next three years played an important part in one of the most exciting periods in the club's history.

He had played against Stoke at Wembley in the League Cup Final of 1972, but had fallen out with Chelsea manager Dave Sexton. He won two full England caps (West Germany and Cyprus, both at home and both victories) and 10 Under-23 caps.

At the start of the 1976-77 season, he fell out with Stoke manager, Tony Waddington, over an injury, and with the Potters short of money

Alan Hudson: One of the most gifted players in the club's history.

following the collapse of the Butler Street Stand roof, he was sold to Arsenal for £200,000 in December 1976.

He had some success at Highbury, picking up a losers' medal in the 1978 FA Cup Final before moving to the United States to play for Seattle Sounders. In 1983 he rejoined Chelsea but never made the first team and Stoke boss, Bill Asprey, then brought him to the Victoria Ground for a second spell for £22,500, which covered Chelsea's costs in bringing him back to this country.

He made a great comeback, helping the club avoid relegation in 1983-84. With the arrival of Mick Mills as manager, he was made captain, but a nagging knee injury forced him to retire at the age of 34. After his football career, he became a night club owner, but now writes a controversial column for a local newspaper.

I

INJURIES

Some players are more injury-prone than others. Perhaps top of the list should come the Potters' most popular defender, Denis Smith. In a Stoke career stretching from 1968-1982, he had five broken legs, four broken noses, a cracked ankle, a broken collarbone, a chipped spine and numerous less serious fractures and cuts!

INTERNATIONAL MATCHES

The Victoria Ground has staged three full Internationals and a Victory International. On each occasion England triumphed. The results were as follows:

Date	Score-line	Attendance
23.2.1889	England 4 Wales 1	3,500
13.3.1893	England 6 Wales 0	6,500*
18.10.1919 (V)	England 2 Wales 0	20,000**
18.11.1936	England 3 Ireland 1	47,882***

* Tom Clare and Joe Schofield played for England
** Charlie Parker (England) and Joey Jones (Wales) played in this Victory International
*** Freddie Steele and Joe Johnston played for England.

INTERNATIONAL PLAYERS

Stoke City's most capped player (i.e. caps gained while players were registered with the club) is Gordon Banks with 36 caps. The following is a complete list of players who have gained full international honours while at the Victoria Ground.

England	Caps	Scotland	Caps
A. Allen	3	T. Hyslop	1
G. Banks	36	W.S. Maxwell	1
A.J. Capes	1	**Northern Ireland**	
M. Chamberlain	8	A. Elder	6
T. Clare	4	R. Irvine	1
C.N. Franklin	27	J. McIlroy	4
T. Holford	1	S.B. McIlroy	26
A. Hudson	2	J. Sheridan	1
E. Johnson	2	S. Smyth	1
J.A. Johnson	5	**Wales**	
A. Lockett	1	G.F. Berry	1
S. Matthews	18	L.E. Davies	4
M. Pejic	4	R.M. James	12
W.S. Rowley	2	W.R. John	6
J.B. Sayer	1	J.L. Jones	1
J.A. Schofield	3	J.T. Jones	10
P. Shilton	3	J. Mahoney	31
G. Shutt	1	S. Meredith	3
F.C. Steele	6	D.S. Nicholas	1
J. Turner	1	Dr L.R. Roose	9
A. Underwood	2	M. Thomas	10
D.V. Watson	2	R.T. Vernon	10
Republic of Ireland		W.M. Watkins	4
G.A. Conroy	27		
B.R. O'Callaghan	7		

Stoke's first player to be capped was Edward Johnson who played for England v Wales at Wrexham on 15th March 1880. The first Scotsman to be capped was Tommy Hyslop against England in 1896. The first Welshmen to be capped were Mart Watkins, Leigh Richmond Roose and Sammy Meredith, all against England in 1902. The first Irishman to be capped was Jack Sheridan against England in 1905. The first capped player for Northern Ireland was Sammy Smyth against England in 1951, whilst the Republic's first capped player was Terry Conroy against Czechoslovakia in 1969.

ISLE OF MAN FESTIVAL

Entering the Isle of Man Soccer Festival for the first time in July 1985, the club beat Manchester City 2-1, an IOM XI 5-0 and Carlisle United 1-0 before losing 0-1 to Blackburn Rovers. Returning to the island the following summer, the Potters beat Hearts 1-0, played out a goalless draw with Bohemians and lost 0-1 to Wigan Athletic at Ramsey. In 1987, the club's three wins and a draw (IOM XI 3-1, Wigan Athletic 2-0, Dundee 1-0 and Hibernian 1-1) brought them the trophy at the third time of trying.

After a three year gap, Stoke re-entered the tournament and remained unbeaten in three games (Motherwell 1-1, Wrexham 2-2 and Blackpool 3-1). They won the tournament again in 1991, beating the IOM XI 7-0, SC Cambuur 2-0 and Sunderland 2-0. They retained the trophy the following season, the last time they have entered, beating the IOM XI 4-1, Wigan Athletic 2-0 and Wrexham 5-1.

J

JOHNSON, TEDDY

A remarkable dribbler with a great turn of speed and a superb shot, he was to become Stoke's first international player when he gained recognition for England against Wales at Wrexham on 15th March 1880. Whilst there are many reference books which show him with Saltley College at this time, he was undoubtedly on Stoke's books and the College's – restrictions were not as strict as they are today. He won his second cap in an 8-1 victory over Ireland in Belfast on 25th February 1884, scoring two goals.

Johnson also won regional representative honours for, amongst others, the Birmingham Association, who awarded him a gold medal for his 'brilliant services' following a game against the London Association. One goal down with just minutes remaining, Johnson dribbled the length of the field to score with a magnificent shot.

JORDAN, JOE

A fearless and wholehearted battler, Joe Jordan gave his all over ninety minutes of every game. Starting his career with Blantyre Victoria, he went to Morton in October 1968 before joining Leeds United for £15,000 some two years later. More of a target man than a goal-scorer, he took some time to establish himself at Elland Road, but scored 35 goals in 169 league appearances. He joined Manchester United in January 1978 for a fee of £350,000 before moving to Italy to play with both AC Milan and Verona. He returned to England to sign for Southampton in a £150,000 deal in August 1984.

A regular choice for Scotland, he won 52 caps and played in the final stages of three World Cups. He scored the goal which took the Scots to the finals in West Germany in 1974.

He became player-coach at Bristol City under his old Leeds colleague Terry Cooper. Later becoming player-manager at Ashton Gate, he took City to the Football League Cup semi-final where they lost 2-1 on aggregate to Nottingham Forest. He moved to take charge of Hearts in September 1990 and led them to runners-up to Rangers in the League. After a brief spell at Celtic, he became Stoke manager and had a 'reasonable' first season in charge. In fact, if he had replaced Mark Stein, the club may have reached the play-offs or even gained promotion! However, after a disastrous start to the 1994-95 season, when Stoke lost three of their opening five League games, including a 4-0 reversal at Bolton, he resigned. He has since returned to Bristol City as manager.

Stoke City's full League record under Joe Jordan was:

P.	W.	D.	L.	F.	A.
36	12	11	13	35	46

L

LARGEST CROWD

It was on Easter Monday, 29th March 1937, that the Victoria Ground housed its largest crowd. A crowd of 51,380 saw Stoke entertain double-chasing Arsenal in a First Division match which ended goalless.

LATE FINISHES

Stoke's latest finish to a Football League season was 14th June 1947 when the club visited Bramall Lane, the home of Sheffield United and lost 2-1.

During the war, many curious things occurred and in 1940-41, the Potters' last match in the Southern Regional League saw them lose by the same score at Leicester City on 7th June 1941, with Harry Bingham scoring from the penalty spot.

LEADING GOAL-SCORERS

The Potters have provided the Football League's leading goal-scorer on two occasions. In 1921-22, Jimmy Broad scored 25 goals to head the Second Division charts, while Freddie Steele scored 33 goals in 1936-37 to top the First Division goal scoring charts.

LEEDS CITY

Founder members of the Second Division in 1892, they were never promoted during their ten seasons. They were expelled from the League in 1919 after making illegal payments during wartime matches. Their fixtures were taken over by Port Vale who, ironically, were expelled from the League for the same reason nearly 50 years later.

The only season that the two clubs met was 1907-08 when the Potters completed the double over their Yorkshire rivals, winning 2-1 at home and 1-0 away.

LEYLAND DAF CUP

A competition designed solely and specifically for Associate Members of the Football League, the Leyland Daf Cup replaced the Sherpa Van Trophy for the 1989-90 season.

Stoke's first game in this competition came the following season when a Paul Barnes goal gave them a 1-1 draw at home to Northampton. However, in their second group match, relegated Mansfield beat them 3-0 to give the Potters an early exit from the Cup.

LOCKETT, HARRY

A great leader of Stoke in its formative years, he was the first secretary of the Football League when it was officially formed in 1888. He soon had to relinquish the secretary's job at Stoke – a position he had held since 1884 – to dedicate himself to his League position. He eventually became a full-time employee, acting as treasurer as well.

However, he repeatedly held on to the League's money for longer than necessary, and instead of banking large amounts as they were received, he deposited them in small portions in various locations. At a meeting on 6th December 1901, he was asked to resign and did so, Lockett did not become an immediate outcast, however. The League continued to pay him occasional sums of money for helping out the new secretary, Tom Charnley. In 1904, he was awarded a League season ticket by the Management Committee. In 1907, however, he tried unsuccessfully and unreasonably to use that season ticket to gain access to the referee's room 'and all parts of the Stoke ground'.

Stoke were then in considerable financial difficulties and Lockett proved to be the man to save them. The Club had been in trouble twice before, in 1892 and 1895, but in 1908, a year after the team had been relegated, apart from the directors, only three Stoke shareholders attended the club's Annual General Meeting. With Stoke suffering from a £1,100 deficit, it was decided to go into liquidation and resign from the League. This aroused so much consternation in the Potteries, that Lockett called a meeting. He announced to a packed audience in the Town Hall that a new company could be formed if twelve men would come forward to meet the liabilities. The target was reached an hour before the deadline, but having resigned from the League,

Stoke couldn't regain their place and so played in the Birmingham League.

Lockett became a director of the club, but in 1911 he filed for bankruptcy, an ignominious fate for a man once regarded as one of the most important personalities in League and local football. Of course, he was also forced to resign from the Stoke board.

Stoke's full League record under Harry Lockett was:

P.	W.	D.	L.	F.	A.
44	7	8	29	53	120

LONG SERVICE

Legend says that Bob McGrory did not like the look of the Victoria Ground, the Potteries or Stoke itself, but after signing from Burnley in April 1921, he stayed with the club as a player and manager for 31 years.

Tony Waddington's association with Stoke City began in 1952 as a coach, and five years later he was promoted to assistant-manager, eventually taking over from Frank Taylor in 1960. He parted company with the club in March 1977, after 25 years service.

Players who have given long service to the club include: Stanley Matthews (1932-47 and 1961-65), Alan Bloor (1961-78) and Eric Skeels (1960-76).

LOSING SEQUENCE

In 1971 and 1972, Stoke City achieved the unenviable record of losing to the same opposition, Arsenal, in successive FA Cup semi-finals.

LOWEST

The lowest number of goals scored by Stoke City in a single Football League season was 24 in 1984-85 when they finished bottom of the First Division. Their lowest points record in the Football League occurred in 1889-90 when only 10 points were secured. The lowest in a 42 match programme was 17 points in the relegation season of 1984-85.

M

MACARI, LOU

Finding it all too easy to win honours with Celtic, he moved south of the border for a new challenge at Old Trafford. He helped United back into the First Division and appeared in three FA Cup Finals for them, collecting a winners' medal when United beat Liverpool 2-1 in 1977. After making 391 appearances, scoring 88 goals for United, he joined Swindon Town as player-manager.

He was sacked in April 1985 after a row with his assistant Harry Gregg, but was reinstated six days later. He steered the club from the Fourth to the Second Division in two seasons. In July 1989 he took over at West Ham United, but lasted only seven months. In January 1990, the FA charged Macari, along with Swindon chairman, Brian Hillier, with unauthorised betting on a Swindon match. For Macari the strain became too much, and after the Hammers had lost 6-0 to Oldham Athletic in the League Cup semi-final, he resigned.

Lou Macari: Current Stoke manager who hopes to guide the Potters into the Premier League.

He returned to management a year later at St Andrew's and took Birmingham to the Leyland Daf Final at Wembley. However, he resigned shortly afterwards, saying the club lacked ambition.

He was soon offered the Stoke City job and at the end of his first season in charge, he had taken the Potters to the Third Division play-offs, where they lost to Stockport

County. Three days later they gained some sort of revenge when they beat the same opponents in the Autoglass Trophy Final at Wembley.

In 1992-93 Macari led Stoke to the Second Division title. They amassed 93 points and suffered only seven defeats.

In early November 1993, he was offered the manager's job at Celtic, but seven months later was sacked by the Parkhead club. Within four months, the likeable Scot was back at the Victoria Ground, being the first manager to return to the club in that capacity.

Stoke City's full League record under Lou Macari is:

P.	W.	D.	L.	F.	A.
194	90	56	48	274	198

McCUE, JOHN

John 'Jock' McCue was a particularly consistent full-back, possessing a fine left foot. There is no doubt that his skill helped him stay in the game longer than most. After playing for Longton Schools, he joined Stoke as a junior before signing professional forms in April 1940. He first played for the club the following month at Tranmere in a War League match. He made his Football League debut against Derby County on 14th September 1946, and was the club's permanent Number 3 for almost fourteen seasons. His final League game, his 502nd, was against Scunthorpe United in March 1960 – a record at the time.

After the war, he came very close to international selection, but had to be content with touring Australia with the FA XI in 1952.

Towards the end of his career at the Victoria Ground, he switched to right-back to accommodate the young Tony Allen. In September 1960, at the age of 38, he signed for Oldham Athletic and although no fee was involved, he made 56 League appearances for the Boundary Park club.

Admired throughout the game for his sporting qualities, he made 675 appearances for Stoke (all games including wartime) – another record.

McGRORY, BOB

Bob McGrory was a Scot who had just finished his apprenticeship as a joiner in a Clydesdale shipyard when he entered professional football. He earned a reputation as a dour and fearless full-back with Dumbarton before Burnley paid £3,000 for his services in August 1920. Disappointed that he was unable to gain a regular place in the Turf Moor side, he moved to Stoke in April 1921.

Bob McGrory: After playing 511 games for the club, he became manager and led them to fourth place in the First Division – the clubs's highest ever position.

One of the most skilful and consistent full-backs of his generation, he made 479 League appearances for Stoke and 32 in the FA Cup – 511 in total, a record that was not to be exceeded for twenty-four years. When he made a comeback for the Potters in 1934-35, he was possibly the oldest player, at the age of 40, to be an ever-present in a season.

Taking over as manager at Stoke in June 1935, following Mather's resignation, he led the club to fourth in the First Division, their highest ever position. He was very active in the transfer market and introduced youngsters of the calibre of Bowyer, Franklin, McCue, Frank Mountford and Johnny Sellars. He had many disputes with Stanley Matthews, who tried to leave the club on a number of occasions. In the last game of the 1946-47 season, Stoke just missed the League Championship – it was won, at the last moment, by Liverpool.

In 1952, after 31 years' service with Stoke, he resigned as manager – his loyalty, judgement, perseverance and tenacity were legendary.

He stayed out of the game until 1954 when he was tempted back into management by Welsh club Merthyr Tydfil who were ambitious for election into the Football League.

Stoke City's full League record under Bob McGrory was:

P.	W.	D.	L.	F.	A.
420	155	102	163	599	633

MAHONEY, JOHN

This Cardiff-born midfielder started his football career at Ashton United before moving to Crewe Alexandra. He made 18 League appearances, scoring five goals for the Gresty Road club, before joining Stoke City for £19,500 in March 1967.

On his arrival at the Victoria Ground, the Stoke coaching staff worked hard on his ungainly style and turned the Welshman into a fine midfield player. He was a substitute when Stoke won the League Cup at Wembley in 1972 and became a regular immediately afterwards, following the sale of Mike Bernard to Everton.

A Welsh international, he won 51 caps to add to his three Under-23 caps.

After George Eastham became manager following Tony Waddington's departure, Mahoney

John Mahoney: A Welsh international, he was substitute when Stoke won the League Cup in 1972.

moved to Middlesbrough for £90,000 before joining Swansea City in his native Wales. He won a Welsh Cup winners' medal with the Vetch Field side in 1981 before moving into non-League management with Bangor City (whom he took into Europe); he followed this by managing Newport County and then Bangor again.

MANAGERS

Following is the complete list of Stoke City's full-time managers and secretary managers, together with the inclusive dates for which they held office. Biographies of all the managers of the club are included in alphabetical order elsewhere in this A-Z:

Tom Slaney	1874-1883	Bob McGrory	1935-1952
Walter Cox	1883-1884	Frank Taylor	1952-1960
Harry Lockett	1884-1890	Tony Waddington	1960-1977
Joseph Bradshaw	1890-1892	George Eastham	1977-1978
Arthur Reeves	1892-1895	Alan Durban	1978-1981
William Rowley	1895-1897	Richie Barker	1981-1983
Horace Austerberry	1897-1908	Bill Asprey	1984-1985
Alfred Barker	1908-1914	Mick Mills	1985-1989
Peter Hodge	1914-1915	Alan Ball	1989-1991
Joe Schofield	1915-1919	Lou Macari	1991-1993
Arthur Shallcross	1919-1923	Joe Jordan	1993-1994
Jock Rutherford	1923	Lou Macari	1994-
Tom Mather	1923-1925		

MARATHON MATCH

It took five games to settle the third round FA Cup tie with Bury. The first match at Gigg Lane ended 1-1 and the replay at Stoke also ended 1-1 and was abandoned after 112 minutes in extra-time. The score at the second replay, at Goodison Park, was 3-3 after extra-time and the third at Anfield ended 2-2 after extra-time. The fourth replay, at Old Trafford on 24th January 1955, ended 3-2 to Stoke after extra-time. It had taken 9 hours 22 minutes to settle the most protracted cup tie between Football League clubs, and 68,383 fans saw the games.

MARSH, JACKIE

Stoke-on-Trent born Jackie Marsh followed other local born players of his generation, such as Bloor, Pejic and Smith, to the accolade of winning a Football League Cup winners' medal at Wembley in 1972.

He made his first team debut in the Stoke side at Highbury on the opening day of the 1967-68 season. Manager Tony Waddington did not want to put too much pressure on the youngster, and even the announcer at the ground was not told the name of City's right-back.

Jackie Marsh: Local born full-back who played in 433 League and Cup games for City.

A fine, strong full-back who could overlap, his flat crosses were an important feature of the club's play in the 1970s. He went on to appear in 433 League and Cup games for the Potters before leaving to play for Hong Kong side, Bulova. He later returned to these shores to play for Northwich Victoria.

MATHER, TOM

When he became Stoke's boss in October 1923, Tom Mather had considerable Football League experience behind him. He worked as assistant-secretary at Manchester City before moving to Bolton Wanderers in a similar capacity. Later he became secretary at Burnden Park, and then secretary-manager in the summer of 1915. All the games played under his charge were wartime fixtures. In the summer of 1920 he became secretary-manager of Southend United.

In his first season in charge at the Victoria Ground, Stoke finished sixth in the Second Division, but due to financial problems, a number of players were not re-signed and others were asked to take a pay cut. In fact, some players turned up at the ground and caused extensive damage to windows and dressing rooms. Wide-ranging reorganization followed, but things began to go rapidly downhill and in 1926 the Potters were relegated to the Third Division (North) for the first time in their history.

However, they bounced straight back, winning the Third Division (North) championship in 1926-27. They narrowly missed promotion to the First Division in 1932, and were promoted as champions a year later.

Tom Mather had become a fine manager who, with few resources, had built a Stoke team to challenge at a higher level. In May 1935, he resigned to take over at Newcastle United, but when war was declared, he left St James's Park. He returned to football in June 1945 as manager of Leicester City, but resigned nine months later.

He ended his career in football as manager of Kilmarnock. In retirement he returned to live in the Potteries.

Stoke City's full League record under Tom Mather was:

P.	W.	D.	L.	F.	A.
495	212	116	167	780	674

MATTHEWS, STANLEY

Known as the "Wizard of Dribble" because of his close ball control, Stanley Matthews was the biggest crowd-puller in the 1950s. Born in Hanley, the son of a boxing barber, he was an outstanding schoolboy footballer, beginning at centre-half, but switching to the right-wing. He then became an apprentice at Stoke City.

He made his League debut for the Potters on 19th March 1932 against Bury at Gigg Lane. In his second season he helped Stoke win promotion to the First Division. The following year, he made his international debut for England against Wales. He won a total of 54 caps, not including wartime and victory appearances for England. His fame grew quickly, fans trooping to matches in their thousands just to watch the "Wizard of Dribble".

Matthews liked the ball played to his feet. Stopping it dead and with perfect control, he would shuffle towards the full-back, teasing him with the ball. The full-back very rarely committed himself, fearing Matthews's reputation. Stan would approach slowly, swaying his body from side to side. The defender would retreat until he thought he knew the direction in which Matthews

Stanley Matthews: The "Wizard of Dribble" knighted for his services to the game.

was going and then lunge for the ball. At this point Matthews would switch the ball to the opposite side and sprint down the wing. However, he was more than just a master of dribble – with just one glance, he could deliver an inch-perfect pass.

When Matthews first asked Stoke for a transfer in 1938, there was a public outcry. Over 3,000 fans attended a protest meeting and another 1,000 paraded outside the ground with placards – he stayed. When he did move on to Blackpool in 1947, however, it was for the bargain price of £11,500.

He played for Blackpool in the 1948 FA Cup Final and was on the losing side, though there was consolation for him in being elected Britain's first Footballer of the Year. It was the same story against Newcastle in 1951. In 1953, with 20 minutes to go, a third losers' medal seemed likely as Blackpool trailed Bolton 3-1. Matthews, however, turned on a brilliant display and tore apart the Bolton defence. Blackpool won 4-3 and the match, one of the greatest seen at Wembley, was hailed as the 'Matthews Cup Final'.

When England entered the first World Cup tournament in 1950, Stanley Matthews was already 35 years old. He had been a League footballer for 18 years and an international for 16, yet he went to Rio and played against Spain. Perhaps even more remarkable, he played in the 1954 finals as well. When England beat Scotland 7-2 at Wembley in 1955, the 40-year-old Matthews made five of the goals. In 1956 he was voted European Footballer of the Year, and was awarded the CBE the following year.

Matthews returned to Stoke in 1961, and the fans flooded back through the gates of the Victoria Ground. He helped Stoke into the First Division. When he played his 701st and last game, against Fulham on 6th February 1965, he was 50 years and 5 days old. He was also knighted that year, the first footballer to be so honoured.

After he retired, he managed Port Vale before going to live in Malta, where he coached Hibernian. He played for a number of local sides and was still sprinting down the wings in his sixties. After living in Canada, he returned to England, and in 1989 became Club President.

There will, of course, never be unanimous agreement on the best player who ever lived, or even the best British player, but one thing is certain, the name of Sir Stanley Matthews would figure prominently in any such discussions.

MAXWELL, WILLIE

Signed from Heart of Midlothian in the summer of 1895, he went on to play in 156 League games over six seasons, scoring 75 goals.

Top scorer for five successive seasons, it was rather surprising that he won only one international cap for Scotland, against England on 2nd April 1898. He did, however, play in a number of Scottish international trial games with the Anglo-Scots against the Scottish League players.

Maxwell was a fiery individual and in 1897 he was suspended by the Stoke club following an unauthorised visit to Scotland. During his time at the Victoria Ground, the club was in financial difficulties and came close to selling him a number of times. He was eventually sold to Third Lanark in 1901 for £250.

Excluding wartime internationals, he was the last Stoke player chosen for Scotland.

He later played for Sunderland, Millwall Athletic and Bristol City where he won a Second Division championship medal. Retiring in 1909, he moved into coaching with Leopold FC in Belgium and also coached the Belgian National side.

MEDICATION

Chosen to play for Stoke City against Sheffield United in an FA Cup tie, Stanley Matthews reported sick with influenza. The Stoke management contacted a specialist in the Royal Infirmary for advice. Matthews was given two capsules. They were pep-pills used by Luftwaffe crews on bombing raids over Britain in the Second World War. They worked perfectly. Stoke won 1-0, but at 9 o'clock that night Matthews was so wide awake that he could have played another ninety minutes!

MILLS, MICK

A naturally left-footed player, Mick Mills joined Ipswich Town after being released by his first club, Portsmouth, when they abandoned their youth policy.

He captained Ipswich and England (winning 42 caps) and played in 591 games for the Suffolk club, scoring 22 goals. During his time at Portman Road, the club won the FA Cup and UEFA Cup. In November 1982, he moved to the Dell and played in over 100 games for the Saints.

In May 1985, he moved to Stoke as player-manager. He arrived at the Victoria Ground when there was little cash to spare and the spectators were staying away. After a number of mediocre seasons, and with the crowd giving him a rough time, he quit and was replaced by Alan Ball.

He later moved to Colchester United who finished bottom of the Fourth Division and lost their League status.

Stoke City's full League record under Mick Mills was:

P.	W.	D.	L.	F.	A.
190	63	58	69	231	261

MOST DEFEATS

Stoke City suffered 31 defeats in 42 Division One matches in 1984-85. Fifteen came from home matches and sixteen were away. They scored in just 17 games.

MOST GOALS IN A SEASON

When Stoke City won the Third Division (North) championship in 1926-27, they scored 92 goals in forty-two matches. They entertained a handful of teams who made unique visits to the Victoria Ground. Ashington were beaten 7-0, with Charlie Wilson scoring five; Durham City lost 4-0; Nelson 4-1; and in the final game of the season, Halifax Town were defeated 5-1.

MOST MATCHES

The most first-class matches played by Stoke City in a single season was 67 in 1971-72. This figure includes twelve Football League Cup, nine FA Cup and four Anglo-Scottish, along with 42 Division One matches. Full-back Jackie Marsh played in 65 of these fixtures.

In the space of four weeks in April 1955, Stoke played nine matches in the Second Division.

Date:	Opponents:	Venue:	Score:
2nd April	Swansea Town	Away	5-3
9th April	Doncaster Rovers	Home	3-0
11th April	Ipswich Town	Home	3-0
16th April	Derby County	Away	2-1
18th April	Rotherham United	Away	1-2
20th April	Doncaster Rovers	Away	1-1
23rd April	Bristol Rovers	Home	2-0
25th April	Port Vale	Away	1-0
30th April	Plymouth Argyle	Away	0-2

However, this pales into insignificance when compared with the club's 1910-11 season. Playing in both the Southern League Division Two and the Birmingham League, the club played twelve games in four weeks!

Frank Mountford: A versatile player who was always in the thick of the action.

MOUNTFORD, FRANK

Born at Askern, to the north of Doncaster, Frank Mountford was brought to the Potteries by his family when he was a very young boy.

He was signed by Stoke when he was still at Bradeley School and first appeared for the club as a centre-forward in wartime football, scoring on his debut at Tranmere in May 1940. In 1940-41, he scored 29 goals and, in fact, played in almost 200 wartime League and Cup games, scoring over 50 goals.

During his playing career he moved back from centre-forward to wing-half then to centre-half and finally to full-back. A versatile player, he would have played anywhere to the club's advantage. However, perhaps his best position was centre-half for he had one of his finest seasons when he replaced Neil Franklin who had gone to Bogota. Frank Mountford was a committed player who was always in the thick of the action and played in such a manner that he regularly required the services of the club trainer.

After 425 League and Cup appearances for the Potters, he hung up his boots and moved back stage to serve the club, first as a trainer, and then as a coach. When the Durban era arrived, he took 'early retirement'.

One of the most formidable of defenders, he never achieved representative honours, having to settle for being one of the best uncapped players around.

N

NELSON

Founder members of the Third Division (North) in 1921-22, they were champions the following season, but were relegated after just one season in Division Two. They spent the remainder of their League career in the Third Division (North) before losing their battle for re-election in 1930-31.

The two clubs first met on 22nd September 1923 when two goals from Harry Davies and one each from Jimmy Broad and Tom Howe gave Stoke a 4-0 win. Nelson gained their revenge a week later, winning their home fixture 2-0. They last met in Stoke's championship-winning season of 1926-27; Stoke winning 4-1 at the Victoria Ground, but going down to the only goal of the game at Nelson.

NEUTRAL GROUNDS

The Victoria Ground has been used as a neutral ground for FA Cup matches on a number of occasions, and as early as February 1889 staged an international match between England and Wales. On 13th

March 1893, the Victoria Ground staged its second international match. Stoke's Joe Schofield played on the left-wing and had a hand in two of the goals as England beat Wales 6-0. The two countries met again on 18th October 1919 in a Victory International. The home side won 2-0. Stoke's Charlie Parker played in this fixture. The Victoria Ground housed its last international match on 18th November 1936 when an England side containing Stoke's Steele and Johnson defeated Ireland 3-1.

In February 1888, the ground was awarded its first FA Cup semi-final when West Bromwich Albion beat Derby Junction 3-0. On 9th November 1895, the Victoria Ground was the venue for a Football League representative game against the Irish League. On 9th October 1911 the ground staged the League's encounter with the Southern League.

On 28th February 1891, Blackburn Rovers beat West Bromwich Albion 3-2 in the FA Cup semi-final at the Victoria Ground, and six years later Everton triumphed over Derby County by the same score-line at the same stage of the competition. The next two FA Cup semi-finals to be held at the Victoria Ground ended at 1-1; they were Bury v Nottingham Forest in 1900 and Aston Villa v Everton in 1905. Newcastle United beat Woolwich Arsenal 2-0 in the 1906 FA Cup semi-final, whilst the last FA Cup semi-final to be played at the Victoria Ground saw West Bromwich Albion beat Bolton Wanderers 2-0 in front of a 49,605 crowd on 20th March 1935.

Stoke City have also had to replay on a neutral ground a number of times:

Date	Opponents	Venue	FA Cup	Score
16.1.1907	West Bromwich Alb.	Villa Park	Rd 1 (2R)	0-2
10.2.1908	Gainsborough.T.	Nottingham	Rd 2 (2R)	3-2
13.12.1909	Exeter City	Fulham	5th Q (2R)	2-1
6.12.1926	Rhyl	Old Trafford	Rd 1 (2R)	1-2
19.1.1931	Manchester United	Anfield	Rd 3 (2R)	2-4
1.2.1932	Sunderland	Maine Road	Rd 4 (2R)	2-1
17.1.1955	Bury	Goodison Park	Rd 3 (2R)	3-3
24.1.1955	Bury	Old Trafford	Rd 3 (3R)	3-2
13.1.1958	Aston Villa	Molineux	Rd 3 (2R)	2-0
6.2.1961	Aldershot	Molineux	Rd 4 (2R)	3-0
8.2.1971	Huddersfield Town	Old Trafford	Rd 4 (2R)	1-0
7.5.1971	Everton	Crystal Palace	3rd Place	3-2

On 5th February 1947, Stoke played Manchester United in the First Division of the Football League at Maine Road as Old Trafford was still recovering from bomb damage. On 17th January 1976, City played Middlesbrough at Vale Park as the Butler Street Stand had had its roof blown off by gale force winds and the Victoria Ground was deemed out of bounds whilst repairs were carried out.

The club's semi-finals were of course played on neutral grounds:

Date	Opponents	Venue	Competition	Score
18.3.1899	Derby County	Molineux	FA Cup	1-3
27.3.1971	Arsenal	Hillsborough	FA Cup	2-2
31.3.1971	Arsenal	Villa Park	FA Cup (R)	0-2
5.1.1972	West Ham United	Hillsborough	F.Lg. Cup (R)	0-0
26.1.1972	West Ham United	Old Trafford	F.Lg. Cup (2R)	3-2
15.4.1972	Arsenal	Villa Park	FA Cup	1-1
19.4.1972	Arsenal	Goodison Park	FA Cup (R)	1-2

The club's two victorious performances at Wembley also qualify. They beat Chelsea 2-1 to win the Football League Cup in 1972, and beat Stockport County 1-0 to win the 1992 Autoglass Trophy.

NEW BRIGHTON

They joined the Third Division (North) when it was extended to 22 teams in 1923-24. The following season they finished third and narrowly missed promotion. The two clubs met in 1926-27 when New Brighton came to the Potteries and earned a point in a 1-1 draw. Josh Williams scored for Stoke. In the return fixture, the Potters produced by far the worst display of their championship-winning season and crashed to a 5-0 defeat!

Having survived a few re-election scares, they eventually lost their battle for League status in 1950-51. In their last season they were top of the table after four games, with maximum points.

NEW GROUND

Situated at Trentham Lakes North, under a mile from the club's Victoria Ground, Stoke City's 28,000 all-seater stadium costing £15.7 million should be completed by 1 August 1997 in time for the 1997-98 season.

NICKNAMES

Many players in the club's history have been fondly known to supporters by their nicknames. This often means just adding a "y" to their name (Doddy, Foxy etc etc . . .) but some Stoke players have had more novel ones. One of the first was Ted Evans who was known as "Jammer", and in November 1892 was the first Stoke player ever to be sent off. Joe Murphy, a half-back signed from Hibernian, was also playing around this time and was known as "Judge" because he played in a wig!

Playing the game in a fiery style, Tommy Holford was known as "Dirty Tommy" in his Stoke days, although he was never sent off.

Albert Sturgess was a popular full-back with a build of 5ft 11ins and 11st 10lbs; he was affectionately dubbed "Hairpin" by the Stoke supporters – nowadays this sort of build would not seem so unusual. Signed from Nottingham Forest in September 1902, Arthur "Sailor" Capes became captain of the Stoke side, and collected an England cap in April 1903.

One of the few players to captain both Stoke and the Vale was Ernest Mullineux. Combining school teaching with his football career, he was known as the "White Nob" because of his hair. Known as "Invincible Dick", goalkeeper Richard Herron was one of the shortest 'keepers to play for Stoke. He managed 18 clean sheets in his 46 appearances, including four Southern League games in succession.

Winning a Third Division (North) championship medal in 1926-27, Bobby Archibald was noted for his superb control and footwork. He was known as "Steve" to his team-mates because of his resemblance to the leading jockey, Steve Donoghue. George Kelly was signed by Frank Taylor for £4,000 from Aberdeen in March 1956. Known to the Boothen Enders as "Grace", he had never played in the Scottish League!

Tony Kelly joined the Potters from Wigan Athletic for £80,000 in April 1986. Known as "Zico", the popular midfielder played for a number of clubs including Colchester, Shrewsbury, Bolton and West Bromwich Albion before returning to Springfield Park. The club's nickname is the Potters, reflecting the importance of the pottery industry in the Stoke-on-Trent area – "the Potteries" – since the nineteenth century.

NON-LEAGUE

'Non-League' is the shorthand term for clubs which are not members of the Football League. Though Stoke provided non-League opposition for a number of League clubs in the FA Cup following their decision to pull out of the Football League, they themselves as a League club have struggled against lesser opposition.

The club's record is:

Date	Opposition	Venue	Score
13.1.1923	Blyth Spartans	Away	3-0
27.11.1926	Rhyl	Away	1-1
2.12.1926	Rhyl	Home	1-1
6.12.1926	Rhyl	Old Trafford	1-2
7.1.1978	Tilbury	Home	4-0
6.2.1978	Blyth Spartans	Home	2-3
17.11.1990	Telford United	Away	0-0
21.11.1990	Telford United	Home	1-0
16.11.1991	Telford United	Home	0-0
22.11.1991	Telford United	Away	1-2
8.1.1994	Bath City	Home	0-0
18.1.1994	Bath City	Away	4-1

NUMBERED SHIRTS

The Football League approved the numbering of players shirts just before the 1939-40 season. Stoke City wore numbered shirts for the first time for a pre-season Football League Jubilee Fund game against Wolverhampton Wanderers on 19th August 1939 which they lost 4-2. Dickie Dorsett scored a hat-trick for Wolves whilst Tommy Sale scored both the Stoke goals.

OSCROFT, HARRY

After Stoke had been beaten 1-0 by Spurs in the third round of the FA Cup on 7th January 1950, manager Bob McGrory approached former City favourite, Freddie Steele at Mansfield about the availability of Harry Oscroft. The Mansfield-born winger signed for Stoke for £8,000 plus Verdi Godwin.

Making his debut against West Bromwich Albion, a week after the FA Cup defeat, Oscroft occupied the Number 11 shirt for nine seasons without interruption. A goal-scoring winger, his 107 goals in 349 League and Cup appearances included a hat-trick against Lincoln City (away 4-1 1954-55), and a best season of 21 goals in 1954-55.

In 1959-60, at the age of 33, he was part of the deal that saw Peter Ford go to Vale Park in exchange for Dickie Cunliffe plus £2,000. After 47 League appearances for Port Vale, he became player-manager at Brantham Athletic, winning a Suffolk Senior Cup winners' medal in 1961-62. He later played the occasional game for Sutton United.

OVERSEAS TOURS

City's first ever trip abroad was in April 1934 when they went to play the Swallows Club in Amsterdam and won 2-1. At the end of the following season, the Potters embarked on a series of three games in Denmark, winning them all. At the end of the 1963-64 season, the club took off on a very demanding tour of Portugal, Colombia, Chile and Argentina. They played in front of some very large crowds with over 80,000 present in Santiago for the game with Universidad of Chile which ended goalless. In Colombia they were beaten 3-2 by Santa Fe, the club Neil Franklin and George Mountford had both played for immediately after the war. At the end of the following season, the club travelled over 20,000 miles to Sweden, Finland and Russia. John Ritchie scored 10 goals in seven games, including four in a 9-1 win over a Finnish XI. Stoke's 3-2 win over Zenit in Leningrad was shown on Russian television!

In May 1969, after flying to the Congo to play a representative side in Kinshasha, they returned via Spain to participate in three friendly games against Barcelona (won 3-2), Pontevidera (lost 0-2) and Granada (won 4-1). At the end of the 1972-73 campaign, the club went 'Down Under' where they played 11 games. Their best victory was an 8-1 thrashing of Otago with John Ritchie scoring all eight goals! In 1976 Stoke made a short tour of Indonesia and Pat Jennings made a guest appearance for the Potters.

On all of their travels Stoke have hit double figures on only one occasion, and that was on their tour of Scandinavia in 1983 when they beat Stromsund 10-1.

P

PEJIC, MIKE

One of the most competitive players ever to wear the red and white stripes of Stoke City. Strong in defence and always eager to attack, he made his first team debut on 8th April 1969 in a goalless draw at West Ham United.

A member of the Stoke side that won the League Cup at Wembley in 1972, he went on to win four full caps for England to go with his eight Under-23 caps.

In February 1977, after 336 League and Cup appearances, the club's desperate financial situation saw him transferred to Everton for £135,000 – a figure which, to the majority of Stoke supporters, was well below his true worth. After 76 League appearances for the Goodison Park club, he moved to Aston Villa, but thereafter his career was hampered by a persistent groin injury that eventually forced him to quit.

After trying his hand at farming and the life of a greengrocer, he returned to the game as coach and manager at Northwich Victoria, Leek Town and Port Vale. Never afraid to put across his point of view, he left Vale and in June 1994 he was appointed manager of Chester City. His stay at the Deva Stadium was short-lived. After just seven months he left the struggling Division Two club.

PELE

The world's greatest player turned out for the Brazilian side Santos in September 1969 as Stoke boss Tony Waddington sought to bring only the best to the Victoria Ground. Disappointingly, only 23,000 turned out to see Santos win 3-2.

PENALTIES

During an 1890-91 FA Cup quarter-final between Notts. County and Stoke at Trent Bridge, a shot was punched off the line by the County left-back, Hendry, when his goalkeeper, Thraves, had no chance of saving it. As the law made no mention of penalties, Stoke had to take a free-kick on the goal-line which Thraves, needless to say, easily smothered. County won the match 1-0 and went on to the final. This incident provoked so much comment that, largely as a result, penalties were finally introduced by the home associations from September 1891. This led to another controversial incident in the following season and Stoke were again the sufferers. They were losing 1-0 to Aston Villa when a penalty was awarded against Villa less than two minutes from time. The Villa 'keeper picked up the ball and booted it out of the ground. By the time it had been found, the referee had blown for full-time! The law was soon changed to allow referees to add on time, specifically for the taking of penalties.

The first player to convert a penalty for the club was Tom Hyslop who scored in the 5-0 win over Sunderland on 14th March 1896. The scorer of the most penalties for Stoke is Frank Mountford who scored from the spot on 14 occasions in the Football League and FA Cup, including five in the 1949-50 season.

Charlie James, who had seven seasons at Stoke, mainly in the reserves, conceded a number of penalties – all for hand ball in the 1913-14 season. The press of the day reporting, 'He just could not resist the temptation.'

Dick Williams was a stylish goalkeeper who made a penalty save on his debut against Lincoln City on 30th April 1927 as Stoke headed towards the Championship of the Third Division (North).

In the 1971 FA Cup semi-final against Arsenal, Stoke's John Mahoney dived full length to push the ball aside as McLintock's header was bound for the net in injury time. Stoke were leading 1-0 and looked to be heading for their first Wembley FA Cup Final, but Peter Storey levelled from the spot to take the tie to a second game which Arsenal won 2-1.

PENALTY SHOOT-OUTS

Quite a recent innovation, the penalty shoot-out is one that football fans either love or hate. The abolition of the penalty shoot-out would certainly not be a loss to the Potters. Their record, set out below, is not a good one!

Season	Competition	Opponents	Scores	Shoot-Out
1970-71	Anglo-Scots Cup	Motherwell	a0-1 h2-1	Lost 3-4
1971-72	FA Cup Play Off	Birmingham C.	a0-0	Lost 3-4
1973-74	Texaco Cup	Birmingham C.	h0-0 a0-0	Lost 1-3
1981-82	Football Lg Cup	Manchester C.	a0-2 h2-0	Lost 8-9
1987-88	Full Members Cup	Leicester C.	a0-0	Won 5-3
1988-89	Football Lg Cup	Leyton O.	a2-1 h1-2	Lost 2-3
1989-90	Full Members Cup	Leeds U.	h2-2	Lost 4-5

PITCH

The Victoria Ground pitch measures 116 yards by 75 yards.

See also 'Victoria Ground' and 'New Ground'.

PLASTIC

There have been four Football League clubs that have replaced their normal grass playing pitches with artificial surfaces at some stage. Queen's Park Rangers were the first in 1981, but the Loftus Road plastic was discarded in 1988 in favour of a return to turf. Luton Town (1985), Oldham Athletic (1986) and Preston North End (1986) followed.

Stoke have played on all four surfaces and although their record on plastic is not a good one, it is probably no worse than that of most clubs. Stoke's first game on plastic was at Loftus Road on 17th January 1984 when they lost 6-0. The only other time they played at Queen's Park Rangers was the following season when they lost 2-0. The club's first goal on plastic was scored by Graham Shaw on 1st March 1988 at Luton Town, but it didn't prevent the Potters from losing 4-1 in the fourth round of the Full Members' Cup. Stoke have played on Oldham's Boundary Park plastic on four occasions, drawing one and losing three. The club's only success on the artificial surface came in their last appearance on Preston's Deepdale ground on 17th October 1992 when, on their third appearance, they won 2-1 with goals from John Butler and Lee Sandford.

PLAY-OFFS

At the end of the 1991-92 season, Stoke played Stockport County in the Division Three Promotion Play-Off semi-final. Losing the first-leg at Edgeley Park 1-0, the Potters could only draw 1-1 at home in the second leg, with Mark Stein scoring Stoke's goal.

In the 1995-96 season, City finished fourth in Division One to reach the play-off stage for a second time. Their opponents were Leicester City. The first-leg, at Filbert Street, ended goalless, though Stoke would have taken an early lead but for the agility of Leicester 'keeper Kevin Poole. He saved with his legs from Simon Sturridge, and clawed away a Graham Potter header that was bound for the top corner.

In the second-leg, the first half was as boring as the first match, but 28 seconds into the second half Garry Parker scored the only goal of the game. City's only effort of note on a disappointing night was Mike Sheron's 20-yard drive that Leicester 'keeper, Poole, collected on his knees.

There were ugly scenes at the end of the game when Stoke supporters poured onto the pitch as the Leicester players were celebrating reaching the play-off finals. Nine police horses were used to drive the supporters back as they tried to reach the Leicester players. The players were trapped in a corner of the ground, surrounded by more police, for ten worrying minutes. Finally, they were given a safe passage to the dressing-room.

PLAYER REBELLION

At the end of the 1923-24 season, some of the Stoke players were not asked to re-sign for the next season, whilst others were asked to accept a cut in their salary. A deputation arrived at the ground by taxi and started to smash the club's offices and dressing rooms, causing a considerable amount of damage.

POINTS

Under the three points for a win system, which was introduced in 1981-82, Stoke's best points tally is the 93 points from 46 matches gained in 1992-93 when the club won the Second Division Championship.

The club's best points tally under the old two points for a win system was 63 points from 42 matches in 1926-27, which would have netted the club 90 points under the present method.

The worst record under either system was the 10 points secured in 1889-90 when the club failed to gain re-election. The club's lowest points total in a season of 42 matches is 17 in 1984-85 when the club were relegated to the Second Division.

POP SONGS

The link between the worlds of popular music and football is not new; fans were purloining tunes from the music halls as early as the late nineteenth century. The arrival of commercial radio in the 1960s undoubtedly accelerated the process. Many hit songs have been enthusiastically taken up by supporters and Tom Jones's 'Delilah' was an instant hit with the Stoke City fans.

When Stoke reached the Football League Cup Final in March 1972, the team had a song written by Tony Hatch and Jackie Trent entitled "We'll be with you". Recorded by the Potters, it reached number 34 in the charts.

PORT VALE

The rivalry between Stoke City and Port Vale stretches right back to the 1883-84 season when the first meeting between the two clubs took place – Stoke winning a friendly game in Burslem 5-3.

The first FA Cup meeting between Stoke and Port Vale was held at the Victoria Ground on 15th October 1887. It was followed by court action. Stoke won the match 1-0, but a few weeks later their goalkeeper William Rowley and another player were sued by Vale for a breach of contract. Stoke had to publish an apology, pay £20 to a Burslem charity, the same amount to Vale for legal fees and release a player to their rivals!

Vale had to wait until the 1889-90 season for their first victory (at any level) over Stoke. That year they won 2-1 at home in a friendly.

On 23rd April 1910, the clubs' reserve sides met at the Victoria Ground to decide the North Staffordshire League championship.

The Vale created something of a sensation by deciding to play former Stoke goalkeeper, Dickie Roose. With Vale leading 2-0 and

Roose in fine form, the Stoke crowd gave vent to their feelings and carried the Welsh international off towards the River Trent.

Luckily for Roose, the local police and Stoke directors intervened and he was saved from a ducking. Afterwards Roose claimed that he did not know the title was at stake, believing it to be a friendly encounter!

On 7th January 1922 Stoke beat Port Vale 4-2 at Burslem in the first round of the FA Cup season. Arthur Watkin grabbed a hat-trick in the game.

During the 1944-45 wartime regional league meetings between the two clubs, Stoke won 8-1 at home and 6-2 at Vale Park within the space of seven days!

In the 1950-51 season, the two clubs met in the third round of the FA Cup. In an entertaining match, Vale went 2-0 up in front of their home crowd, but two goals by Albert Mullard, who was later to join the Vale, gave Stoke a 2-2 draw. There was another tremendous match in the replay when a Frank Bowyer goal in the 88th minute settled the tie in Stoke's favour.

The record League gate for a match between Stoke and Port Vale is 40,066 at Vale Park on 25th April 1955. Stoke won 1-0, with Frank Bowyer again finding the net.

The clubs met three times in Cup competitions in 1992-93. Vale came out on top, winning 3-1 at home in the first round of the FA Cup after a goalless draw at the Victoria Ground, and 1-0 in the Southern Area semi-final of the Autoglass Trophy. In the 1995-96 season, Vale completed the double over the Potters, winning both League matches 1-0.

PROFESSIONALISM

In the season of 1885-86, with Abraham Fielding as Chairman, Stoke entered the professional ranks with broken-time payment to seven players. They were Philip Birch (goalkeeper); Tommy Clare and Edgar Mountford (full-backs); Ted Smith and George Shutt (half-backs); and Alf Edge and Bernard Rhodes (forwards). Each player received half-a-crown (12p) per match.

Some senior players went on strike as the club tried to introduce a differential payment scheme, but in the end the club decided to increase everybody's payment by 100 per cent to 5s (25p).

The FA scorned professionalism and only accepted it in 1885 when they realised there was very little they could do about it.

PROGRAMME

The price of the official programme in 1952 was 3d (three old pence), equivalent to just over one new penny! It was not at all like today's glossy match programmes, being printed in black text throughout except for the red and white cover. By 1963 programmes cost one shilling (5p) and by 1972, metrication and inflation pushed the price up to 10p. In 1989, programmes finally reached the £1 level.

PROMOTION

Stoke have won promotion on six occasions. They won promotion to the First Division in 1921-22 as runners-up to Nottingham Forest, although 11 home draws and one defeat cost them the championship. There was an unbeaten League run, which stretched from a 2-1 Boxing Day defeat at Fulham to a 3-2 Good Friday reversal at Blackpool – 15 games undefeated, including nine wins. The club's top scorer was Jimmy Broad with 25 goals, including four in a home win over Crystal Palace (5-1), the first such achievement by a Stoke player.

P.	W.	D.	L.	F.	A.	Pts.
42	18	16	8	60	44	52

The club's next experience of promotion was in 1926-27 when the club went up as champions of the Third Division (North). They were on top of the League all the way through the season, achieving ten 'doubles' over their opponents. Charlie Wilson equalled Broad's League record of 25 goals.

P.	W.	D.	L.	F.	A.	Pts.
42	27	9	6	92	40	63

In 1932-33 the club were promoted as champions of the Second Division, creating numerous records in the process. Joe Mawson was top scorer with 16 goals, despite missing the last ten games of the season with an untimely injury. Manager Tom Mather paid £2,000 for the services of Reading's Jack Palethorpe and he scored eight goals in the run-in to secure promotion.

P.	W.	D.	L.	F.	A.	Pts.
42	25	6	11	78	39	56

The club 'officially' celebrated its centenary in 1962-63, and at the same time won promotion as champions of the Second Division.

Despite failing to win any of the first six games of the season, they then remained unbeaten in 18 League games before losing to Leeds United just before Christmas. There then followed one of the worst winters on record and the club had to wait until early March before resuming League football. Tony Waddington signed Irish international Jimmy McIlroy from Burnley, but his debut ended in disaster as Stoke lost 6-0 at Norwich. However, the club then strung together six successive wins and despite three successive defeats, promotion was gained when the Potters beat Luton 2-0.

P.	W.	D.	L.	F.	A.	Pts.
42	20	13	9	73	50	53

Stoke started the 1978-79 season well, winning five of their first six League games to go top of the League. The season came to a climax on the final Saturday when Stoke visited Meadow Lane to play Notts. County. The Stoke supporters went wild when Paul Richardson headed the only goal of the game to take the Potters back into the First Division.

P.	W.	D.	L.	F.	A.	Pts.
42	20	16	6	58	31	56

The club last won promotion in 1992-93, after losing in the play-offs the previous season. On 21st November, Stoke beat Blackpool 3-1 at Bloomfield Road to go top – a position they held until the end of the season. Playing some delightful football, they embarked on a tremendous run of 25 League games without defeat to create a club record and set up the championship.

P.	W.	D.	L.	F.	A.	Pts.
46	27	12	7	73	34	93

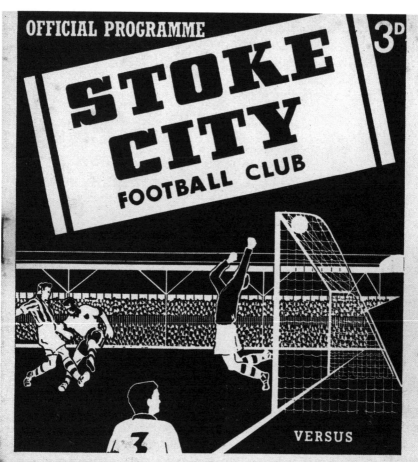

CENTENARY
CELEBRATION
MATCH
1863-1963

STOKE CITY v REAL MADRID

WEDNESDAY, 24th APRIL, 1963   Price: ONE SHILLING

Q

QUICKEST GOAL

The times given for goals are notoriously unreliable, particularly as you go back to earlier years, but playing against West Bromwich Albion Reserves on 30th October 1909, Amos Baddeley netted what could well be the quickest goal ever scored by a Stoke player. Without a West Bromwich player touching the ball, Baddeley scored after just eight seconds. Unfortunately, Stoke lost the game 3-1.

R

RAPID SCORING

When Stoke City beat Swansea Town 6-2 on 9th December 1957, the Potters produced a magnificent first half display to score five goals inside half an hour. Stoke took the lead in the tenth minute when Frank Bowyer shot home from 30 yards. Three minutes later, Johnny King made it 2-0 after receiving Dennis Wilshaw's defence-splitting pass. Stoke's third goal came in the 26th minute when Kelly followed up Bowyer's powerfully struck shot which the Swansea 'keeper had failed to hold. A minute later, Kelly scored his second and Stoke's fourth goal when he turned in Bowyer's pass.

Allchurch pulled a goal back for the Swans before Kelly completed his hat-trick in the 40th minute with a long range drive. King added another in the second half, but it was Stoke's first half performance that will live long in the memory.

REAL MADRID

The club chose to celebrate its 'Centenary' in 1963 by arranging a friendly match against Real Madrid, without doubt the greatest club side in Europe. A crowd of 44,914 turned out on 24th April to see the fixture. It was a magnificent occasion with three of the world's all-time greats on the field: Ference Puskas, 'The Galloping Major'; Alfredi di Stefano, a legend amongst number nines; and Stoke's Stanley Matthews who, although 48, still had the support and affection of two generations of football fans.

Real took the lead after 16 minutes when Ruiz shot from outside the Stoke penalty area to completely wrong-foot Jimmy O'Neill in the Potters' goal. Within three minutes of the second half starting, Dennis Viollet had cut in from the right wing to place the ball just inside the post for the equaliser. The Victoria Ground erupted four minutes later when Jimmy McIlroy's shot deflected off Muller to give Stoke the lead. Stoke substitute Ron Andrew had come on to the field and it was he who upended the great Puskas in the penalty area. The Hungarian-born number ten scored from the spot to level the scores. The Spanish side then took the initiative and for the last thirty minutes bombarded the Stoke goal, but despite hitting the woodwork twice, they couldn't snatch a winner and the match ended at 2-2.

RECEIPTS

The club's record receipts are £109,000 for the Rumblelows Cup second round, second leg match against Liverpool on 9th October 1991. This provides a contrast to 9th November 1885 when the club set a receipts record when Preston North End were the visitors. The top club of the day beat Stoke 1-0. The receipts for the game totalled £114 12s 3d, which was more than the receipts for the next four home games added together!

RE-ELECTION

Finishing bottom of the Football League in 1889, Stoke, together with the three clubs immediately above them, had to apply for re-election. Stoke finished top of the poll with 10 votes and, therefore, comfortably secured a second season in the League.

However, as bottom team again in 1890, the club were once more obliged to seek re-election. Both Burnley and Notts. County had sought re-election after the first season, but on this occasion it was Stoke who lost out to Sunderland.

REEVES, ARTHUR

Replacing Joseph Bradshaw as Stoke's secretary-manager in January 1892, he soon realised that he faced a formidable task as the club finished next to the bottom of the First Division in his first season in charge. After much hard work on his part, Stoke climbed to mid-table security in 1892-93. Reeves had gambled by giving local-born players such as Clare, Rowley and Underwood their debuts and signing some Scottish imports. It worked, but, unfortunately, in 1893-94 the club's performances did not match the previous seasons and he was replaced by Bill Rowley.

Stoke's full League record under Arthur Reeves was:

P.	W.	D.	L.	F.	A.
97	35	15	47	181	210

REFEREES

According to Stoke's official programme in December 1904, certain referees were given appointments "not through merit but through favouritism and because they are particular nominees of some member of the committee". Since the article had already criticised a Mr Stott of Rawtenstall, the inference was quite clear: Charles Sutcliffe, the little lawyer from Rawtenstall who drew up all the referee appointments, was abusing his position.

Though angered by this suggestion, instead of castigating Stoke, the management committee began to watch Mr Stott's performances. Stoke had been right. He was struck off almost immediately, and the committee drew up a new system for choosing match officials.

RELEGATION

The club have suffered relegation on seven occasions. The club's constant flirtation with relegation eventually proved disastrous in 1906-07 when Stoke were bottom of the League from New Year onwards. There was a shortage of goals throughout the season and 28 players were used in all, including four amateurs. Stoke ended the season with 26 points – five away from safety.

The club's second relegation experience came in 1922-23 when they could manage only two draws from their first eight games of the season. Anchored firmly to the foot of the table, they rallied slightly in the New Year with the arrival of a few new faces, but relegation could not be averted.

In 1925-26, the first season under the new offside law, Stoke were badly hit by injuries and did not share in the high scoring generally seen around the country. Relegation to the Third Division (North) for the first time in the club's history looked inevitable from Christmas onwards and, against the background of the General Strike, the inevitable happened!

Stoke's next experience of relegation was in 1952-53. After slipping into the relegation zone, the club managed seven games without defeat at the turn of the year, but this progress was not maintained and everything hinged on the final game of the season against an already-doomed Derby County at the Victoria Ground. Thomson missed a penalty and Stoke lost 2-1 to join the Rams in the Second Division after twenty years in the top flight.

The club's fifth taste of relegation was in 1976-77 when Tony Waddington's replacement, George Eastham, turned to youth to get them out of trouble. It failed, and on Monday 16th May, 1977 at Villa Park, Stoke lost 1-0 to a controversial 10th minute penalty and were relegated.

The club's sixth and most disastrous of relegation seasons was 1984-85. Stoke broke almost all the records – fewest points, most defeats, fewest goals scored – the season could not end quickly enough!

The club's final experience of relegation was in 1989-90 when they finished bottom of the Second Division, winning only six of their 46 League games and scoring just 35 goals.

RIOT

Riots at St Andrew's on 29th February 1992 caused the Third Division match between Birmingham City and Stoke City to be delayed for half an hour. It was announced that the game was abandoned, but after the ground was cleared the managers agreed to play out the last 60 seconds and the two sides just kicked the ball to each other until the referee blew for time.

The trouble began within seconds of Paul Barnes's equaliser for Stoke in injury time. About 400 angry Birmingham supporters swarmed on to the playing area and made towards the Stoke end. One of them, who was later identified and arrested, hit the referee.

John Ritchie: The club's most prolific goal-scorer with 171 goals.

RITCHIE, JOHN

The most prolific goal-scorer in Stoke City's history with 171 League and Cup goals, he was signed from Kettering on a scout's recommendation for £2,500. Making his debut against Cardiff City on 13th April 1963, he went on to score 59 goals in 91 appearances in his first two seasons. He took a particular liking to Sheffield Wednesday, hitting his first hat-trick against them in a 4-4 draw in 1963-64. The following season he scored all four goals in City's 4-1 win over the Owls. In fact, in November 1966 he joined the Hillsborough club in a £70,000 deal. The Stoke supporters were absolutely amazed that such a proven goal-scorer had been allowed to move. To his credit, manager Tony Waddington acknowledged it was a mistake. However, he rectified that mistake in August 1969 when he re-signed Ritchie for £25,000 to team him up with Jimmy Greenhoff. During his time at Wednesday, he was called into the Football League side and scored twice in a 7-2 win over the League of Ireland.

On his return to the Victoria Ground, he once again led the Stoke forward line with distinction, and in 1972 won a League Cup winners' medal at Wembley. Playing at Ipswich on 24th September 1974, he fractured his leg – it was his last game for the club and apart from the occasional game for Stafford Rangers, it ended his career. It enabled him to concentrate on his pottery business which was just a short distance from the Victoria Ground.

ROWLEY, WILLIAM

Stoke's first League goalkeeper and their first England international goalkeeper, he was a converted centre-forward, having played in that position for Hanley Orion. He had played for the Stoke Swifts, the club's reserve side, in 1883-84, but then joined Burslem Port Vale. It was only on rejoining Stoke that he built his reputation. As soon as he did, however, Vale won a County Court action against Rowley, preventing him playing for Stoke. The club also had to pay £20 to a Burslem charity. Stoke's neighbours claimed that the Potters had induced Rowley to join them. One of Rowley's last games for Vale had been against Stoke and he had broken two ribs. However, he was eventually allowed to sign for Stoke and went on to give great service.

In 1895 he became Stoke's secretary, but still turned out in an emergency when required. When secretary he was certainly not conventional, and even bought players out of his own pocket! His period in charge was full of controversy and in 1898 he transferred himself to Leicester Fosse, including a signing-on fee for himself! After only one appearance for them, the FA intervened and refused to transfer his registration. Both the Leicester secretary and Rowley were suspended for twelve months.

Stoke's full League record under William Rowley was:

P.	W.	D.	L.	F.	A.
60	26	3	31	104	106

RUTHERFORD, JOHN

One of Newcastle United's most accomplished forwards, he gained three League championship medals and played in five FA Cup Finals for the Magpies. He scored 90 goals in 336 games for Newcastle before joining Arsenal where he played in 255 games, scoring 31 goals. He worked in munitions in World War One, but still continued to turn out for the Gunners.

He was transferred to Stoke as player-manager in March 1923, but stayed for only a few weeks before a row with a director saw him make a quick exit. He had been unable to play at the start of the 1923-24 season due to his involvement in a motor accident and when he was fit to resume his duties, there was little or no money available for new players. After his spell at the Victoria Ground (the Potters won 2, drew 2 and lost 2 of his six games in charge) he rejoined Arsenal and was persuaded to come out of retirement to play for Clapton Orient (later, Leyton Orient) in 1926.

S

SCHOFIELD, JOE

Like many of his generation, Joe Schofield was introduced to football through the Church. Joining the club from Hanley Hope Sunday School, he made a goal-scoring debut against Burnley on 10th October 1891. Wearing the centre-forward's shirt, he scored in each of his first three games, but it was as an outside-left that he made his name. A regular in the Stoke side for seven seasons, he won three England caps against Ireland and Wales (twice), scoring one goal. He also represented the Football League against the Irish and Scottish Leagues.

On and off the field, Joe Schofield was always the perfect gentleman, but in 1899 ill health forced him to retire and he became a schoolteacher.

When the club reformed after going bankrupt, he became a director and was Honorary Secretary during the war. In January 1919, he became secretary-manager at Port Vale, and was manager at his untimely death in 1929.

SECOND DIVISION

Stoke City have had seven separate spells in the Second Division.

Relegated at the end of the 1906-07 season, they started their first campaign in the Second Division in disastrous style, collecting just one point from their first four games. Though they dropped into the bottom two, they did improve and eventually finished ninth. However, within the club, finance was now a major problem and though Chairman W.A. Cowlishaw made strenuous last-ditch efforts to rally support, he failed. He pulled Stoke out of the League and put the club into liquidation. It was only their success in winning the Southern League in 1914-15 that prompted the club to seek election to the Football League at the Annual General Meeting on 19th July 1915. Duly reinstated, they had to wait until the 1919-20 season before they achieving any measure of success. Though they started the campaign well, collecting maximum points in eleven of their first fifteen matches, they tailed off to finish the season in mid-table. The following season, 1920-21, saw them slip perilously close to relegation, but in 1921-22 the club achieved an unbroken League run of 15 wins from 27th December to 8th April inclusive and gained promotion.

Relegated at the end of their first season back in the top flight, Stoke endured two traumatic seasons, culminating in their drop into the Third Division (North) for the first time in the club's history.

Promoted back to the Second Division at the first attempt, the club had a good season in 1927-28, finishing fifth. After finishing mid-table for a couple of seasons, the Potters were in the hunt for promotion throughout the 1931-32 season, but just missed out and finished in third place. However, they did not have long to wait for the following season they took the Second Division title in style with many records being created – the best away record, the best defensive record and the best goal average in the top two divisions.

The club's fourth spell in the Second Division began in season 1953-54, following relegation from the top flight the previous season. It was to be the club's longest stay in this Division, ten seasons in all. They finished fifth in seasons 1954-55, 1956-57 and 1958-59 before winning the championship in 1962-63, even though they failed to win any of their first six games.

Fourteen seasons of First Division football followed before a disappointing season in 1976-77 resulted in City returning to the Second Division. Fortunately, two seasons later the club returned to the top flight, finishing in third place, a point ahead of Sunderland. There then followed six seasons of First Division football before the disastrous campaign of 1984-85. Relegated with fewest points, most defeats and fewest goals scored, City were back to the Second Division.

There followed five seasons of mediocrity before the club suffered the ignominy of relegation to Division Three in 1989-90 – the first time since 1927.

With the governing bodies altering the structure of the Divisions and introducing a new Premiership, Stoke again found themselves playing in the 'Second' Division in 1992-93. It was a season in which they played some delightful football and after beating Blackpool 3-1 at Bloomfield Road in November, they hit the top spot and stayed there. They ended the season as the new 'Second' Division champions with 93 points, three more than runners-up, Bolton Wanderers.

Stoke's all-time record in the Second Division is:

P.	W.	D.	L.	F.	A.
1312	524	332	456	1993	1724

SECRETARIES

The first secretary of Stoke, taking office in the late 1860s, was a headmaster named John Whitta Taylor. During the early part of this century, however, the position was usually undertaken by the team boss whose official title was secretary-manager. It was only when Bob McGrory took over as manager from Tom Mather in June 1935 that Tom Hancock was appointed as the club's first official secretary.

The club's present secretary is Mike Potts who has been a magnificent servant at the Victoria Ground, having been initially appointed in July 1973 as assistant to Hancock.

SELLARS, HARRY

When Harry Sellars signed for Stoke from Leadgate Park in December 1923, he was to start a long association between the Sellars family and the Victoria Ground.

Initially, he played for Darlington as an amateur. The club arranged a job for him – cleaning windows in railway carriages! He turned professional with Leadgate Park in 1922, turning down the chance of a trial with Manchester United.

A wholehearted player at left-half or inside-left, his strengths were his accurate passing and good covering in defence. He won a Second Division championship medal with the Potters in 1932-33, but a couple of years later he injured his knee and never really regained his form and fitness. After 394 first team appearances, he left Stoke for Port Vale in July 1937.

He later became landlord of The Crewe Arms in Middleport and was tempted out of retirement to help Congleton Town win the Cheshire Senior Cup.

Assistant-manager to Bob McGrory at Stoke and later manager of Irish club Dundalk, his son John followed him into the Stoke side.

SELLARS, JOHN

He joined the club in 1941. In addition to his football abilities, he was also a professional sprinter, having won the prestigious English Powderhall Sprint.

He made his debut for the club in War League football during the season of 1942-43, though he was mainly a part-time professional, combining his appearances for Stoke City with his chosen profession as a shoe designer for the Lotus Shoe company in Stone.

His first game in the Football League was after football was formally restored following the Second World War. Stoke won, beating Preston North End 5-0 on 1st February 1947.

John Sellars: Son of Harry Sellars, he had to retire with a serious eye injury after 413 first-team appearances for City.

An attacking and hard-working wing-half, he was also considered to be Stoke's number one utility player, having played in every position except centre-half and goalkeeper.

Serving the Potters very much in the same tradition as his father, Harry Sellars, had done before him, he made 413 first team appearances. His last appearance came in the fifth round of the FA Cup against Bolton Wanderers at a rain-swept Burnden Park on 15th February 1958 when Stoke lost 3-1.

Though he had to 'retire' with a serious eye injury, there were hopes of a return, but he failed to make the first team again and his career finally ended in 1960.

SEMI-FINALS

Stoke's first appearance in a semi-final came in 1898-99 when they lost 3-1 to Derby County at Molineux in the FA Cup. Derby's Steve Bloomer scored a magnificent hat-trick. The club had to wait sixty-five years before making their next bow at that stage of a competition. The Football League Cup had been introduced in 1960, and until 1963-64 Stoke had made little impact. Reaching the two-legged semi-finals, the Potters beat Manchester City 2-0 at home with goals from Ritchie and Asprey. Although they lost 1-0 at Maine Road, they were through to the Final. In 1970-71, the club reached their second FA Cup semi-final against Arsenal at Hillsborough. Goals from Smith and Ritchie put Stoke 2-0 up, but Arsenal's Peter Storey hit home two late goals to take the game to a replay. This time the venue was Villa Park, but with Storey again performing miracles, the Gunners won 2-0.

Stoke's next appearance in a semi-final was in 1972 when they played West Ham United in the Football League Cup. It was a two-legged affair and as Stoke lost 2-1 at home, their chance seemed to have gone. However, at Upton Park a John Ritchie goal levelled the tie and was to earn a replay. Three minutes from the end of extra-time, West Ham were awarded a penalty. Gordon Banks made a brilliant save from Geoff Hurst's spot kick and the contest went to a third tie. A crowd of 46,916 witnessed a goalless draw and so the two sides made the trip to Old Trafford for a fourth encounter. In a game either side could have won, it was City who took the honours, winning 3-2 with Terry Conroy grabbing the winner.

That season Stoke also played Arsenal again in the FA Cup semi-final. The tie was at Villa Park and although Stoke drew 1-1, thanks to an own goal from Arsenal's Peter Simpson, they failed to impress. The following Wednesday they lost the replay 2-1 at Goodison Park.

In 1973-74, goals from Hurst, Pejic, Conroy and Greenhoff gave City victory by 4-1 over Bristol City in the semi-final of the Watney Cup – a trophy they won, beating Hull 2-0 in the Final.

In 1991-92, Stoke played Peterborough United in the semi-final of the Autoglass Trophy. After drawing 3-3 in the first leg at the Victoria Ground, the prospect of winning through to Wembley looked diffi-cult. However, a goal from Paul Ware at London Road gave the Potters victory, 4-3 on aggregate.

The last time the club reached the semi-final stage of a competition was in 1992-93 when they lost 1-0 to rivals Port Vale in the area semi-final of the Autoglass Trophy.

SHALLCROSS, ARTHUR

Arthur Shallcross played for Leek before becoming a Football League referee in 1895. Appointed manager of Stoke in February 1919, he did not endear himself to the club's supporters when he sold Charlie Parker to Sunderland in October 1920. In fact, the Potters avoided relegation by only the narrowest of margins in 1920-21 when they finished twentieth. With money to spend on new players, he was able to strengthen his squad and signed future manager Bob McGrory.

In 1921-22 the Potters finished runners-up to gain promotion to the First Division, but spent only one season in the top flight, being relegated at the first attempt. In April 1923 Shallcross resigned and was never seen in League Football again.

Stoke's full League record under Arthur Shallcross was:

P.	W.	D.	L.	F.	A.
162	56	41	65	211	219

SHILTON, PETER

Although Stoke fans never really saw Peter Shilton at his best, he was undoubtedly one of the greatest goalkeepers of the modern era.

He made his Football League debut for Leicester City as a 16-year-old and progressed to the point where he put manager Matt Gillies under pressure to either play him, at the expense of Gordon Banks, or let him go.

In November 1974, after he had made 286 League appearances for the Filbert Street club, he joined Stoke for £325,000, a world record fee for a goalkeeper. He trained as hard as any and his dedication to fitness was second to none. However, following the club's relegation in 1976-77, he played in three Second Division matches before being transferred to Nottingham Forest. At the City Ground under Brian Clough, he won a League Championship medal, 2 European Cup winners' medals, Football League Cup winners' and runners-up medals and a European Super Cup medal.

Peter Shilton: Signed from Leicester City for £325,000 – a record fee for a goalkeeper.

After Forest, he served Southampton and Derby County before becoming player-manager at Plymouth Argyle. No player in the sport's history has appeared in more Football League matches than Peter Shilton.

Awarded the MBE, he is England's most capped player with 125 international appearances to his name. He was unfortunate to have been around at the same time as Ray Clemence, and one can only speculate how many caps he would have won if he had been alone and unchallenged.

SIMOD CUP

The Simod Cup replaced the Full Members' Cup for the 1987-88 season. The Potters produced a fine run in the new competition, beating First Division opposition in Portsmouth (Away 3-0) and Sheffield Wednesday (Away 1-0). They then disposed of Leicester City in the third round 5-3 on penalties after the game had been goalless. The club went out of the competition in the next round, losing 4-1 at Luton Town. The following season, Stoke travelled to Southampton and were well beaten 3-0.

In 1989-90, goals from Berry (penalty) and Bamber saw Stoke beat Bradford City 2-1. Facing Yorkshire opposition again in Leeds United in the second round, the Potters went out 5-4 on penalties after the game had ended all square at 2-2.

SKEELS, ERIC

Having been associated with Stockport County as an amateur, he wrote to Stoke City asking for a trial. The trial went very well, and in December 1958 he signed for the Potters as a 19-year-old professional. He had to wait until 12th March 1960 before making his debut in a 3-1 home defeat by Charlton Athletic. After that, he became established and had 18 years at the Victoria Ground, winning a Second Division championship medal in 1962-63 and a runners-up medal in the 1963-64 League Cup. It was a great pity that when the club finally reached Wembley in 1972, Eric wasn't in contention for a place.

Eric Skeels: 'Mr Dependability' who holds the club appearance record with 592 League and Cup games.

Known as "Mr Dependability", Eric Skeels holds the club appearance record with 592 first team League and Cup games to his name. Essentially a midfield player, he was also so adaptable that he would play anywhere. He made his last appearance in a Stoke shirt on 21st February 1976 before joining neighbours Port Vale on a free transfer in September of that year, when he was almost 37. After just five appearances for Vale, he signed for Leek Town. He kept a pub in the area for a number of years and is still a regular visitor to Stoke's home games.

SLANEY, THOMAS

Tom Slaney trained as a teacher at Saltley College and was a leading figure not only at the Stoke club, but to football generally in the area. A schoolmaster at St John's, he was appointed the club's secretary-manager in 1874, a position he held until 1883. He continued to play during his time in office and, in fact, was club captain from 1875 to 1882.

He was credited, with Harry Allen, with being instrumental in the formation of the Staffordshire FA, of which he was also secretary.

Synonymous with the club in those amateur days, he became a first-class referee when his playing days were over.

SMITH, DENIS

Idolised by the Stoke public for his total commitment, he overcame countless injuries and broken bones to establish himself in the number five shirt, which he was to make his own.

He graduated from Queensbury Road School, through Stoke-on-Trent Schoolboys into Stoke's apprentice ranks. He made his City debut against Arsenal at Highbury on 14th September 1968. It wasn't long before he won a regular place alongside Alan Bloor at the heart of the Stoke defence. Not the most cultured of defenders, there were, nonetheless, not too many strikers who enjoyed playing against him. There are a number of stories about his playing days that will live in the club's football histories and legends.

Denis Smith: The most committed of all Stoke players, he overcame a number of injuries to make 407 League appearances for the Potters.

There was the occasion when the trainer came on to

the pitch to be told by Denis that he thought he had broken his leg, to be told by the trainer that he should know...he had broken it enough in the past!

On 23rd February 1974 he scored the winning goal against Leeds United as Stoke came from two goals down to win 3-2 and end the Elland Road side's record breaking run of games without defeat.

Though he represented the Football League, a full international cap eluded him. However, he won a winners' medal in 1972 as City lifted the League Cup.

Towards the end of his playing career, he joined the Potters' coaching staff and earned a well-deserved testimonial from the club.

After leaving Stoke, he embarked on a successful career in management, which took him to York City, Sunderland, Bristol City and his current club, Oxford United.

Frank Soo: The first player of Chinese descent to play in the Football League, he won seven caps for England.

SOO, FRANK

The first player of Chinese descent to play in the Football League, he was very popular with the spectators and noted for his artistry and trickery.

A Liverpool schoolboy, he became a clerk and drifted into non-League football with West Derby Boys' Club and Prescot Cables before joining Stoke. He played his first game for the club on 6th November 1933, a 6-1 defeat at Middlesbrough.

Ranking amongst the country's greatest half-back lines in the pre-War period, he appeared in perhaps the most famous Stoke half-back line of all-time, Tutin – Turner – Soo. During the wartime period he finally won international recognition, winning seven caps for England in sides that contained his Stoke colleagues Franklin and Matthews.

As the war came to a close, he did not always agree with Stoke boss, Bob McGrory, and he joined Leicester City who were then managed by Tom Mather, the former Stoke manager. He later played for Luton Town and Chelmsford City.

On retiring from the game, he went into coaching and coached the Israeli national side as well as having spells in Scandanavia and Italy. In this country, he has managed Scunthorpe United and St Albans.

SOUTHERN LEAGUE

The club's first team operated in the Southern League Division Two (Western Division) in 1909-10, winning all ten of their matches. They began the season with an 11-0 home win over Merthyr Tydfil, and followed it with an 8-1 home victory over Ton Pentre and a 7-1 success at Burton United.

Their record was:

P.	W.	D.	L.	F.	A.	Pts.
10	10	0	0	48	9	20

As champions of the Western Division, they played Hastings St Leonards, winners of the Eastern Division, on 25th April 1910 for a Championship match. Stoke triumphed 6-0. In those days not all the Southern League sides completed their fixtures and five games in Stoke's section were not played. Despite their performance, Stoke were not promoted.

The following season saw Stoke finish second in the Southern League Division Two and gain promotion. The club strengthened their first team squad for the 1911-12 season in the First Division of the Southern League. After only a moderate start and then three heavy defeats in the space of five days over Christmas, the club dropped into the bottom five. However, new signings were brought in and the club turned in a strong second half of the campaign to finish mid-table. There were high hopes for the following season, but by Christmas the club had hit the bottom of the League and stayed there.

The 1913-14 season saw Stoke competing in the Second Division of the Southern League against a number of poor Welsh clubs and southern sides such as Brentford, Croydon Common and Luton Town. Starting with nine straight wins, the crowds flocked back to the Victoria Ground, but once this great run was stopped, Stoke slipped back to end the season in fifth place.

The following season opened against the threat of war, with many Welsh clubs considering playing to be unpatriotic. Despite losing their first game 2-1 at Mardy (who resigned halfway through the season and had their record expunged), Stoke led the table virtually from the start and had wins of 10-0 over Ebbw Vale and 8-0 over Mid Rhondda on their way to the title.

SOUTHPORT

Southport's Football League career lasted from 1921-22, when they were founder members of the Third Division (North), until they failed to gain re-election in 1977-78 when they lost their place to Wigan Athletic on a second ballot. The two clubs met in Stoke's 1926-27 Third Division (North) championship-winning season with the Potters completing the double over their Lancashire opponents, 4-0 at home and 3-0 away.

SOUTH SHIELDS

They joined the Second Division as South Shields Adelaide in 1919, but subsequently dropped the word Adelaide from their name. It was in 1930-31 that they moved to Gateshead and adopted their new name. The two clubs met on fourteen occasions, with the north-east side generally having the upper hand. Stoke had to wait until their sixth meeting, on 5th September 1921, before recording their first win. The Potters only other successes came in 1927-28 when South Shields were relegated, Stoke winning 3-1 at home and 3-2 away.

They spent the rest of their time in either the Third Division (North) or Fourth Division before failing to be re-elected in 1959-60, despite finishing third from the bottom of the Fourth Division, six points ahead of bottom club, Hartlepool United.

SPENCER, BILLY

Spotted playing for Hebden Bridge in the Yorkshire West Riding League, he joined Stoke as an amateur in December 1924. Turning professional four months later, he made his debut in the 2-1 win over Portsmouth on 13th February 1926.

A good full-back, he was cool and calm under pressure and had very sound positional sense. A contemporary of the great Bob McGrory, the full-backs were said not to get on, but the Nelson-born defender always denied it. After 354 first team appearances, he was restricted to reserve team outings, and in June 1938 he joined Crewe Alexandra.

During the war, he played in the same battalion as his old Stoke team-mate, Harry Davies. When the hostilities ended, he ran the Compasses public house in Newcastle-under-Lyme before returning to his home town as a warehouseman. He was coach to Lancashire Combination side Nelson for a number of years before his deafness forced him to quit.

SPONSORS

The club's first sponsors were Ricoh in the 1981-82 season. They also had a second spell in October 1983, when the Potters were looking elsewhere! The first time their name re-appeared on the players' shirts was in front of the BBC TV Cameras when City beat West Ham United 3-1. In the mid-eighties, the club announced a very lucrative sponsorship deal with H and R Johnson Tiles (Cristal Tiles).

The 1990-91 season saw the team finish in its lowest ever position in the Football League – 14th in Division Three – and this with another new club sponsor in Fradley Homes. The club's next sponsors were Ansells who signed a two-year deal at the outset of the 1991-92 season. In the summer of 1993, Carling were signed up as the club's new sponsors. Broxap and Corby Ltd took over for the 1995-96 season.

SPORTING POTTERS

Left-winger Louis Page (1919-1921)who scored 22 goals in 122 League games for Northampton, and 111 in 248 games for Burnley after his spell at the Victoria Ground, played Baseball for England. Harry Ware

(1930-1935) was a boxer (his father was British Champion)and swimmer. George Kell (1956-1958) teamed up with Johnny King (1953-1961), a fine tennis player who was on the fringe of playing at Wimbledon.

City have also had a number of fine athletes on their books such as Harry Connor (1953), the last amateur to play for the club; Freddie Steele (1934-1959), who hurdled for Staffordshire; and Johnny Sellars (1947-1958) who was a formidable sprinter in Powderhall events.

STAFFORDSHIRE COUNTY CUP

For the 1877-78 season, the Staffordshire FA offered a County Cup for which interested clubs could compete. The Stoke club beat Talke Rangers 1-0 to become the first winners. On their way to the final they beat Mow Cop 26-0. Stoke, in fact, retained the Cup the following season, beating Cobridge 2-1. They next won the trophy in 1913-14, beating Walsall 4-2 at Hanley. Prior to this, they had appeared in seven finals. In 1882-83, when they lost 3-2 to West Bromwich Albion, they scored 42 goals in reaching the final. After 1914, games in the Staffordshire Cup were mainly fulfilled by Stoke City's reserve or youth teams.

STEELE, FREDDIE

An outstanding schoolboy footballer, Freddie Steele was snapped up by Stoke City in 1931 and worked in the club offices until he was old enough to sign professional forms. He made his League debut for the club on 22nd December 1934 in a 4-1 win at Huddersfield. Although he played in nine matches that season, it was 1935-36 before he established himself.

Despite standing only 5ft 10ins tall, he possessed remarkable heading ability and thrived on the nickname of 'Nobby'. On 23rd September 1936 he made his debut for the Football League, scoring in a 3-2 defeat against the Irish League in Belfast. Three weeks later he made his debut for England at full international level against Wales, that being the first of six caps that season. The critics placed him just behind the immortals, Dixie Dean and Tommy Lawton. He scored eight goals in his six internationals, seven of them in his last

Freddie Steele: Holder of the club record for the most goals in a season with 33 in 35 appearances in 1936-37.

three games – England's tour of Scandanavia at the end of the 1936-37 season.

In that season of 1936-37, he hit 33 League goals from just 35 appearances – still a club record.

When the war broke out, Freddie Steele was 23 and had scored 90 goals in 135 games for Stoke. At the outbreak of hostilities he had knee surgery for the first time, but was able to play in 95 wartime games, scoring 81 goals!

When one considers that he missed seven seasons because of the war and innumerable matches through a recurrence of knee injuries, his career record is all the more impressive. He scored 140 League goals in 224 appearances, and a further 19 goals in 27 FA Cup ties.

In June 1949, at the age of 33, he left Stoke to become player-manager at Mansfield Town. He later returned to the Potteries to manage Port Vale (twice!) with success.

STOKE RAMBLERS

The club was formed in 1868 by two old Carthusians, Henry John Almond and William Macdonald Matthews, who had just left school to be apprentices at the railway works. The Ramblers' first game was on 17th October 1868 when a team mainly made up of railway company employees drew 1-1 with Mr E.W. May's Fifteen. The game was played on the Stoke Victoria Cricket Club ground. The Cricket Club's secretary, Mr J.W. Thomas, was also the first honorary secretary of the Ramblers. Stoke retained the title of Ramblers for two years before dropping the name and becoming known merely as Stoke.

SUBSTITUTES

Substitutes were first allowed in the Football League in the 1965-66 season. The first appearance of a substitute in League football came at Burnden Park when Charlton Athletic's Keith Peacock came on during Bolton Wanderers' 4-2 win. Stoke City's first substitute was Keith Bebbington who came on for Dennis Viollet in the club's opening game of the season, a 2-1 defeat away to Arsenal.

The first goal-scoring number twelve was John Mahoney who scored for City in their 1-0 win over Leicester City at the Victoria Ground on 24th August 1968.

Under the single substitute rule, the greatest number of substitutes used by City in a single season was 29 in 1982-83, but since 1986-87 two substitutes have been allowed, and in 1994-95 the club used 65.

The greatest number of substitute appearances for Stoke were made by Carl Saunders who came on during 34 League games before his move to Bristol Rovers. It was in 1990-91 that Nyrere Kelly, better known as Tony, caused the City records on the matter of substitutes to be rewritten, with an extraordinary 13 League appearances in the number twelve shirt.

SUNDAY FOOTBALL

The first-ever Sunday matches in the Football League took place on 20th January 1974 as a result of the three-day week imposed by the government during its trial of strength with the coalminers. Two weeks prior to that, Stoke's third round FA Cup tie at Bolton was switched to Sunday 6th January. Bolton won 3-2 with John Byrom grabbing a hat-trick. Stoke's scorers were Ritchie and Haslegrave.

On Sunday 27th January, Stoke entertained Chelsea in front of a 31,985 crowd – the first ever Division One game played on a Sunday. Stoke won 1-0 with Geoff Hurst scoring the all-important winner from the penalty spot, just nine minutes from time.

SUSPENSIONS

The 1898-99 season did not begin well when three of Stoke's players were suspended for a breach of club rules during pre-season training exercises.....they drank champagne!

Peter Dobing's disciplinary record was such that he was to serve a record nine week suspension – which was hardly a punishment as he broke his leg at Ipswich Town, effectively ending his career.

SUSTAINED SCORING

In Stoke's highly successful season of 1926-27 when the club won the Third Division (North) championship, Charlie Wilson scored 19 goals in 12 games, including five in the 7-0 thrashing of Ashington.

During 1945-46, the first season of League football after the war, Freddie Steele scored 15 goals in the first ten games of the campaign, including hat-tricks in the 5-4 defeat at Middlesbrough and the 3-0 win over Sheffield United.

John Ritchie scored 13 goals in nine games in the middle of the 1963-64 season, including a hat-trick in an exciting 4-4 draw at home to Sheffield Wednesday. In more recent times, Wayne Biggins scored 12 goals in 12 games at the start of the 1991-92 season.

SWEETINGS FIELD

Stoke moved to Sweetings Field, which was owned by Alderman Sweeting (Mayor of Stoke), in 1875. Here, as many as 200 spectators would attend, paying first one penny and then two pence to watch their idols. The club stayed at the ground until the merger with the Stoke Victoria Athletic Club in 1878 when they played on the Athletic ground.

T

TAYLOR, FRANK

Frank Taylor made 56 appearances at full-back for Wolverhampton Wanderers before the outbreak of the Second World War. He played in their surprise 4-1 defeat by Portsmouth in the 1939 FA Cup Final.

He also gained a wartime cap for England against Scotland at Hampden Park in April 1944. England won 3-2 in front of 133,000 fans.

He was forced to retire from the game through injury at the age of 28 and immediately joined the Wolves training staff. He was appointed manager of Scarborough in June 1948, and later became Major Frank Buckley's assistant at Hull. He did a similar job at Leeds before becoming Stoke's manager in June 1952.

One of the new breed of track suit managers, he set great store by fitness. He put a sign up in the Stoke dressing room which read, "Are you 90 minutes fit? It's the last 20 minutes that count – train for it!" However, at the end of his first season in charge, the club were relegated. Throughout the 1950s, the Potters remained a mid-table Second Division side. He was shocked when he was sacked by the new chairman, Albert Henshall, in 1960, but the Stoke board had shown a great deal of patience with his management.

Stoke City's full League record under Frank Taylor was:

P.	W.	D.	L.	F.	A.
336	138	69	129	560	504

TELEVISION

When the world's top players arrived at the Victoria Ground on 28th April 1965 to play in Stanley Matthews's farewell match, television cameras and Eurovision beamed the night's entertainment to an estimated audience of 112 million!

At the end of that season, the club undertook a tour to Sweden, Finland and the Soviet Union, appearing on Russian television!

Stoke were featured in a 'live' match on television for the first time, via B Sky B's Sport Channel, on 21st November 1990. They played Telford United in an FA Cup first round replay at the Victoria Ground. Lee Sandford scored the only goal of the game to give Stoke a 1-0 win.

TESTIMONIALS

On 28th April 1965, the world's best players turned up to bid Stanley Matthews goodbye. Television cameras and Eurovision beamed the night to an estimated audience of 112 million people who saw Stoke beat the Matthews XI 6-4.

On 12th December 1973, over 20,000 fans turned up at the Victoria Ground for Gordon Banks's testimonial game. In a match played in torrential rain, a Stoke side including Eusebio and Bobby Charlton lost 2-1 to Manchester United.

TEST MATCHES

Stoke were involved twice in the Test Matches. Firstly, in 1894-95 they finished third from the bottom of Division One and their place depended on a game against the third from the top in Division Two. That game saw them pitted against Manchester United on a neutral ground – Burslem. Stoke won 3-0, thanks to two goals from Joe Schofield and another from Jack Farrell.

The club were involved a second time in 1897-98, and it was their final game which brought about the system's downfall. In those days it was customary for the bottom two clubs of the First Division and the top two of the Second Division to play 'Test Matches' to decide which two should be numbered among the sixteen clubs of the First Division. There was no automatic promotion and relegation as we know it today.

On Thursday 28th April, Blackburn had beaten Newcastle 4-3, leaving both Stoke and Burnley on four points and Newcastle on two points. Stoke and Burnley players knew, therefore, that a draw in their match at the Victoria Ground on the following Saturday would be sufficient to keep Stoke in the First Division and lift Burnley out of the Second.

Despite the fact that everyone knew an 'arrangement' was in the offing, Stoke and Burnley made their intentions so patently obvious that they gave the League no choice but to revamp the 'Test Match' idea or drop it completely. "The game proved a complete fiasco," reported "The Staffordshire Advertiser". "Athletic News" called it a fraud. "The teams could have done without goalkeepers so anxious were the forwards not to score." Played in wet and windy conditions on a shocking pitch, the players kicked the ball into the crowd so often that the disgruntled fans "gave themselves up to unlimited fun with the ball on their own account". To stop this happening for the umpteenth time, one of the linesmen tried so hard to stop the ball reaching the crowd that he ran headlong into a policeman who went head over heels!

The results were as follows:

Newcastle United 2	Stoke 1	Blackburn 4	Newcastle United 3
Stoke 1	Newcastle United 0	Newcastle United 4	Blackburn 0
Burnley 2	Blackburn 0	Burnley 0	Stoke 2
Blackburn 1	Burnley 3	Stoke 0	Burnley 0

The final table read:

	P.	W.	D.	L.	F.	A.	Pts.
Stoke	4	2	1	1	4	2	5
Burnley	4	2	1	1	5	3	5
Newcastle United	4	2	0	2	9	6	4
Blackburn Rovers	4	1	0	3	5	12	2

TEXACO CUP

The predecessor of the Anglo-Scottish Cup, it was launched in 1970-71 and was for English, Irish and Scottish club sides not involved in European competitions.

The club's first opponents in the competition were Motherwell. After losing 1-0 at Firs Park, goals from Bloor and Burrows gave Stoke a 2-1 win. In the ensuing penalty shoot-out, City lost 4-3 with Burrows, Conroy and Bernard scoring from the spot. The Potters gained revenge the following season after drawing Motherwell again. A Mike Bernard goal gave them victory in the away tie while two goals from John Ritchie and one apiece from Jimmy Greenhoff and Sean Haslegrave gave them a comfortable 4-1 home win. Their next opponents were Derby County, but despite a good showing at the Baseball Ground, the Potters lost 3-2. The return match was a hard fought affair with Denis Smith scoring for Stoke in a 1-1 draw in front of 23,461 spectators.

The club entered the competition for the last time in 1973-74, but went out 3-1 on penalties to Birmingham City after both games had ended goalless.

THIRD DIVISION

Stoke were relegated to the Third Division for the first time in their history at the end of the 1925-26 season. However, there was never any real doubt that the club would win promotion back to the Second Division at the first attempt. Charlie Wilson equalled Jimmy Broad's scoring record of 25 League goals in a season, and Harry Davies scored 15.

Stoke were on top of the League throughout the campaign and achieved ten doubles over their opponents. After beating Accrington 1-0 on 23rd April 1927, the Potters took the championship, eventually finishing with a five point lead over their nearest challengers.

The club's next season in the Third Division was 1990-91 when they finished in their lowest-ever League position of 14th. The following season, under Macari's leadership, the club made the play-offs, only to be denied a final place by Stockport County. Deeply disappointed at missing out on promotion, the club found themselves playing in and winning the Second Division the following season after the governing bodies had altered the divisional structure.

Stoke City's full playing record in the Third Division was:

P.	W.	D.	L.	F.	A.
134	64	35	35	216	148

TRANSFERS

The transfer of players has always been a feature of football, though in the early days some unusual arrangements were made.

In 1896 Stoke were involved in one of the most bizarre of transfer moves when they signed Darwen's Allan Maxwell. The fee was a set of wrought-iron gates, which the club provided for Darwen's ground.

On 16th April 1932, Stoke City visited Ashton Gate to fulfil the Second Division fixture against Bristol City. The Robins, bottom of the table, were in such financial difficulties that they offered Stoke any player in their side for £250 cash. Stoke snapped up winger Joe Johnson who went on to play for England five years later. The fastest instance of paying off a transfer fee was probably the Potters' purchase of the veteran Stanley Matthews in October 1961. On 14th October, Stoke drew 1-1 at home with Preston North End in Division Two and attracted a crowd of 8,409; a fortnight later they beat Huddersfield Town 3-0 in another Division Two game before 35,974. In the interim they had signed Matthews and the extra receipts at his first home game more than repaid his £2,800 transfer fee from Blackpool.

The club's first £100,000 signing was ex-Leeds United star Jimmy Greenhoff from Birmingham City in the summer of 1979. When Geoff Hurst joined Stoke City in July 1973 he was asked for reasons by one interviewer and replied, "Firstly, I won't have to play against Denis Smith. Secondly, so I don't have to take penalties against Gordon Banks." In 1974, Stoke paid £350,000 (the highest fee ever paid for a player in English football) when they signed Peter Shilton from Leicester City. The same year they paid £250,000 for Alan Hudson from Chelsea.

When Mark Stein left the club for Chelsea in October 1993, the Potters received their record transfer fee of £1.5 million. The largest amount paid by the club was in July 1989 when they parted with £480,000 to acquire the services of Ian Cranston from Sheffield Wednesday.

TURNER, ARTHUR

Playing his football for Wolstanton PSA and Downings Tileries, he was working as an upholster when he signed as an amateur for West Bromwich Albion. He never made the first team at the Hawthorns, and when he lost his job, he applied for a position at Stoke. He signed as an amateur in November 1930, but was quickly moved to full professional forms.

Playing in arguably the club's best-ever half-back line of Tutin – Turner – Soo, he captained the side for a number of seasons. Between 27th April 1935 and 12th March 1938, he played in 118 consecutive games for the club. Following the emergence of Billy Mould, the Stoke board allowed Turner to sign for Birmingham City, but within six months of his signing for the St Andrew's club, war was declared. Turner guested for Crewe, Wrexham and Stoke during war football, but when the hostilities ended he resumed his League career with Southport.

He retired in 1949 to become Crewe Alexandra's manager, but a year later moved to Stoke as assistant-manager to Bob McGrory. In

1954 he joined Birmingham City as boss and led them to Wembley two years later. He left the Blues in 1958 and took over at Oxford United (they were known as Headington United when he arrived)and led them into the Football League in 1962. He guided them to promotion in 1965 and then to the Championship of the Third Division in 1968.

UEFA CUP

Goals from Conroy, Hurst and Ritchie provided a comfortable 3-1 home win over Kaiserslautern, a little known West German side, on 13th September 1972. This was expected to take the Potters through to the next round. In the second leg, Farmer was in goal for the injured Banks and Eric Skeels preferred to Ritchie in a more defensive line-up. Unfortunately, Stoke were easily defeated 4-0, and to make matters worse, Ritchie who came on to replace Bloor was immediately given his marching orders for striking an opponent.

The following year, the club's opponents in the competition were Ajax of Amsterdam. In the first leg at the Victoria Ground, the Dutch side's possession football out-manoeuvred the Potters, though Denis Smith levelled Ruud Kroll's goal for the visitors. Making just one change for the second leg in Holland, Hurst for Conroy, Stoke played superbly to hold the Dutch side to a goalless draw. Sadly, Stoke were out of the competition on the away goals rule.

UNCHANGED TEAM

Between 14th November 1931 and 6th February 1932, the club had a 14-match unbeaten run and manager Tom Mather was able to pick the same Stoke side for sixteen weeks – a club record. The team was: Lewis, McGrory, Beachill, Robertson, Turner, Sellars, Liddle, Bussey, Mawson, Sale and Archibald.

UNDEFEATED

When Stoke City drew 0-0 at home with Bolton Wanderers on 5th September 1992, they began a sequence of 25 unbeaten matches in Division Two – a club record. They lost 1-0 to Leyton Orient on 27th February 1993. During the run they won 17 and drew eight games to set up the championship.

UTILITY PLAYERS

A utility player is one of those particularly gifted footballers who can play in several or even many different positions.

Probably Stoke's earliest utility player was Bob Ramsey, the scorer of the club's first hat-trick in the Football League. In his eighteen months with the club he turned out at left-back, wing-half, centre-forward and outside-left.

Johnny Sellars was a manager's dream for his adaptability and commitment. He could play at full-back or centre-forward, though the majority of his games were played at wing-half.

After about the mid-1960s, players were encouraged to become more adaptable and to see their roles as less stereotyped. At the same time, however, much less attention came to be paid to the implication of wearing a certain numbered shirt and accordingly, some of the more versatile players came to wear almost all the different numbered shirts at some stage, although this did not necessarily indicate a vast variety of positions.

Eric Skeels, Stoke's Mr Dependability, was certainly talented enough to wear all City's outfield shirts except number five during his career at the Victoria Ground. Alan Dodd also wore every outfield shirt with the exception of number nine in his two spells with Stoke.

In recent years, both Carl Saunders and Paul Ware have worn every outfield shirt.

V

VALE PARK

On 17th January 1976, Stoke played Middlesbrough in a Football League Division Two match at Vale Park after a storm had ripped off the roof of the Butler Street Stand, making the Victoria Ground out of bounds whilst repairs were carried out. Ian Moores scored the only goal of the game with just three minutes remaining.

On 26th April 1976, Port Vale celebrated their centenary with a game against Stoke at Vale Park; the match ended all-square at 1-1.

VICTORIA GROUND

Stoke is not only the second oldest club in the League, but has been in continuous occupation of its present ground longer than any other Football League club, having been at the Victoria Ground since March 1878.

The ground took its name from the nearby Victoria Hotel which now occupies the site of the club's first main ground, Sweeting's Field. The ground, being an athletics venue, was initially oval in shape and built to accommodate a running track. Both ends had open banking with one small wooden stand on the East Side (Boothen Road).

Stoke's first game at the Victoria Ground was a friendly against Talke Rangers on 28th March 1878 which Stoke won 1-0 in front of a 2,500 crowd.

Although they were founder members of the Football League in 1888, they had to drop out of the competition two years later, only to win back their place after twelve months. The club suffered relegation in 1907, and at the end of the next season, the club went out of the Football League and were not re-admitted until 1919.

When the club returned to the Second Division, the Victoria Ground had been improved. There were two good stands and another small wooden stand, seating 1,000, which was opposite the main stand. Between the present day Boothen Stand and Boothen End was a small hut for the players' dressing rooms. A main feature of this hut was an old stove around which the players would assemble after winter games!

During the early 1920s, a new, but still mainly wooden, Main Stand was built alongside this hut, with seating for 2,000 spectators. In 1930, the Boothen End of the ground was terraced and later covered, and so the original oval shape of the ground was lost.

In 1935, the Butler Street Stand was built. This had seating for

The Victoria ground

5,000 with a small paddock in front and at each end. The barrel roof curled around the corners. On 29th March 1937 the ground housed its highest attendance when 51,380 packed into the Victoria Ground for the visit of Arsenal in a First Division match. During the Second World War, the Butler Street Stand was used as an army camp.

The Victoria Ground's first floodlights were switched on in October 1956 for a match against Port Vale. Four years later work began on modernising the stadium.

Another new Main Stand was built in three stages, the last one coinciding with the club's return to the First Division in 1963. The 1970s were great years for Stoke as they reached two FA Cup semi-finals and entered Europe, but it was not all smooth progress as over the weekend of 3rd/4th January 1976, a gale blew off the roof of the Butler Street Stand. The club had to play one game at Vale Park, but were soon able to replace the roof with a neat white cover.

In October 1979, the Stoke End Stand was opened at the ground. It was a two-tier stand with 4,000 seats above the paddock. Consequently, two of the original floodlight pylons had to be replaced. There are now two pairs of different sized floodlight pylons at the Victoria Ground – the only instance of its kind in the Football League.

In 1983 the surviving corner of the old Butler Street Stand was taken down, and in 1987 the Stanley Matthews Suite was officially opened by the great man himself. In July 1994, the Stoke board announced plans for a new 9,000 seat Butler Street Stand. Work commenced in May 1995.

VICTORIES

In a Season:

City's greatest number of victories in a season is 27, achieved in seasons 1926-27 and 1992-93 when the Third Division (North) and Second Division championships were respectively secured.

In a Match:

City's best victories in the major competitions are as follows:

Home

Football League	10-3 v West Bromwich Albion	1936-37
FA Cup	10-1 v Caernarvon Wanderers	1886-87
Football League Cup	6-2 v Chelsea	1974-75

Away

Football League	6-0 v Bury	1953-54
FA Cup	5-2 v Wigan Borough	1925-26
Football League Cup	4-2 v Bristol Rovers	1971-72

WADDINGTON, TONY

One of the most respected managers in the game, Tony Waddington gained a reputation for giving ageing stars who were nearing the end of their careers an 'Indian Summer'. He was at the Victoria Ground for twenty-five years as third team coach, assistant-manager and manager. He held the manager's job for seventeen years. For most of his time in charge, Stoke were a First Division club, and they also won their first major trophy in 1972 when they beat Chelsea in the League Cup Final at Wembley.

Waddington joined Manchester United as an amateur in 1941, whilst serving in the Royal Navy. Playing at either full-back or wing-half, he moved to Crewe Alexandra in 1946, but six years later was forced to retire from the game through a knee injury.

He arrived at Stoke in 1952 as coach, and five years later was promoted to assistant-manager. In June 1960 he succeeded Frank Taylor as manager and introduced new tactics, a new style of play and several new players to the Stoke supporters. He signed 46-year-old Stanley Matthews from Blackpool for £3,000 to help the team win promotion from the Second Division. Another Waddington masterstroke was the signing of Burnley's Jimmy McIlroy for £25,000 in that promotion-winning season of 1962-63. His teams gained a reputation

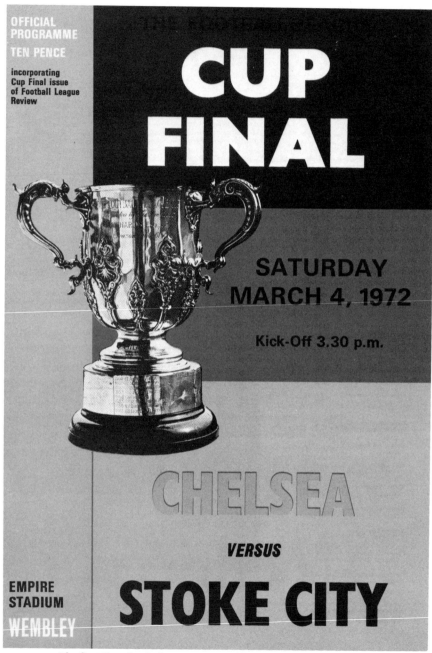

The first time that Stoke went to Wembley – with Tony Waddington.

Tony Waddington: 'Mr Stoke City', he was one of the most respected managers in the game.

as 'veterans' teams' as he signed players such as Eddie Clamp, Alex Elder, David Herd, Roy Vernon and Dennis Viollet. He also signed England's goalkeeper, Gordon Banks.

The Stoke manager also brought the club a reputation for entertaining and successful football. In 1964 the Potters reached the final of the League Cup, but lost 4-3 to Leicester City on aggregate. They also reached the semi-finals of the FA Cup in 1971 and 1972, losing to Arsenal on both occasions. His major triumph came in 1972 when the club reached Wembley for the first time. They played in Europe for the first time the following season, but with the departure of most of their leading players in 1976-77 the club were relegated, and in March 1977 Waddington left.

Referred to by many as 'Mr Stoke City', he returned to management two years later with Crewe, but in July 1981 he left. He was appointed Associate Director of Stoke City in the summer of 1993, a position he retained until his death on 29th January 1994.

Stoke City's full League record under Tony Waddington is:

P.	W.	D.	L.	F.	A.
701	241	197	263	924	948

WAR

Stoke have lost a number of players while they were on active service. During the First World War, the following met with untimely deaths – Dick Herron, Henry Hargreaves, Stan Ripley, Walter Nixon, Tom Kinson, George Limer and Jack Shorthouse.

The famous Dr Leigh Richmond Roose was also killed in action during the First World War. The former Stoke favourite died in 1916 (he also won the Military Medal). Presumably, this is why Stoke lent their efforts to the North Staffords' Comfort Fund.

WARTIME FOOTBALL

First World War

For the whole of the First World War football period, Stoke played in the Lancashire section. In 1915-16 they ended the season in mid-table, whilst they finished third the following year. In 1917-18 they were winners of the Lancashire section and so qualified to play Leeds City (winners of the Midland Section) for the League Championship Cup. The first leg, at Leeds on 4th May 1918, was lost 2-0, and though Stoke won the second leg 1-0 seven days later, Leeds took the Cup on aggregate. It had been a tremendous season for Stoke as they won their first nine games of the season. Blackburn Rovers were made to suffer as Stoke beat them 16-0 at home and 8-1 away!

In the 'final' War season, Stoke ended their season in the Lancashire section as runners-up to Everton.

Second World War

In contrast to the events of 1914, once war was declared on 3rd September 1939, the Football League programme of 1939-40 was immediately suspended and the government forbade any major sporting events. Consequently, for a short while there was no football of any description. Stoke had opened the season with a 4-0 thrashing of Charlton Athletic, followed by a 2-1 home defeat by Bolton Wanderers. On 2nd September they drew 2-2 at Middlesbrough with Tommy Sale scoring both goals.

After a series of friendly matches, Stoke's campaign in the Western Regional League started on 21st October 1939 with a 4-4 draw at

Goodison Park against Everton. The club's top scorer was Tommy Sale with 20 goals in 21 League games. Stoke won the League, two points clear of Liverpool. Frank Mountford scored on his first team debut that season and netted a hat-trick in his second. This game was at home to Notts. County on the opening day of the 1940-41 season in the South Regional League. The game also saw an 18-year-old centre-half by the name of Neil Franklin make his debut. The season was haphazard, with the teams not playing the same number of matches. The following season saw Stoke involved in two separate series of the 'North' League and War Cup competition. Tommy Sale scored 55 goals in total as the matches provided goals in abundance. In 1942-43, the club were beaten in only 12 of their 48 games. Whilst they did not do so well the following season, they were defeated only once in the Qualifying Competition and reached the knockout tournament, where they lost over two legs to Aston Villa. Tommy Sale was reaching the twilight of his career, but was still top scorer with 35 goals in 1944-45. In the season Stoke beat Port Vale 8-1 and 6-2 in a seven-day spell!

Whilst the 1945-46 season saw the reinstatement of the FA Cup, the regional leagues continued with Stoke having to settle for a mid-table position. It was also during the wartime football that the Burnden disaster occurred on 9th March 1946.

WATNEY CUP

This was Britain's first commercially sponsored tournament, and was a pre-season competition for the top two highest scoring teams in each division of the Football League the previous season. They could only compete if they had no other European involvement.

Stoke won the competition in 1973-74, the last time it was played. After victories over Plymouth Argyle and Bristol City, they beat Hull City 2-0 in the final with both goals from captain Jimmy Greenhoff.

WEATHER CONDITIONS

In February 1873, Stoke visited Nottingham to play Forest on a frozen pitch. To assist their grip on this surface the Forest players added nails to their boots and 'ripped Stoke players to shreds'. Keeping two players 'loitering' in the Stoke area, Forest ran out winners 3-1.

On 15th February 1890, Stoke played at Wolves in the third qualifying round of the FA Cup. The game was played in driving sleet and on a very heavy ground, with Wolves winning 4-0. Stoke protested and the game was ordered to be replayed the following Saturday. Unfortunately, Stoke went down again, this time by 8-0!

In January 1976, a blustery storm and gale force winds contrived to blow the roof off the Butler Street Stand. The Victoria Ground was closed for a time whilst repairs were carried out. Neighbours Port Vale offered Stoke the use of their ground, and on the one occasion they used it, they beat Middlesbrough 1-0 with Ian Moores scoring the winner just three minutes from full-time.

WIGAN BOROUGH

They spent ten full seasons in the Third Division (North) and had a best finish of fourth place in 1928-29. They resigned on 26th October 1931 and their results were expunged from the League. The two clubs met only in Stoke's triumphant championship winning season of 1926-27 – the Potters winning 2-0 at home and 3-0 away.

WORST START

The club's worst ever start to a season was in 1951-52 when it took twelve League games to record the first victory of the season. Losing ten and drawing one of their first eleven matches, they eventually beat Burnley 2-1 at the Victoria Ground with goals from Martin and Siddall. The Potters made a similar start to the 1989-90 season, drawing eight and losing three of their first eleven matches before defeating WBA 2-1 on 17th October 1989.

X

XMAS DAY

There was a time when football was usually played on Christmas Day, but in recent years the football authorities have dropped the fixture from their calendar. The last time Stoke City played on a Christmas Day was in 1954 when they beat Bury 3-2 at home, courtesy of a Johnny King hat-trick.

YOUTH CUP

Stoke first competed in the competition in 1952-53, losing 7-0 at West Bromwich Albion in their first match – still their heaviest defeat. They did not compete the following season, but in 1954-55 they defeated Kidderminster Harriers 14-1 to record their biggest win in the competition. That campaign saw them reach the semi-finals, only to lose 2-1 over two legs to West Bromwich Albion. They reached the semi-finals again in 1960-61, but lost 5-2 on aggregate to Everton. They fought their way through to the semi-finals for a third time in 1983-84 and beat Arsenal 6-2 over the two legs. Playing in their first-ever FA Youth Cup Final, they drew the first leg against Everton at Goodison Park 2-2 with Howells and Sutton the scorers. They were unable to take advantage of playing on home soil in the second leg, losing 2-0 to the Merseyside outfit.

ZENITH DATA SYSTEMS CUP

The Zenith Data Systems Cup replaced the Simod Cup for the 1989-90 season. City's first match in this competition saw the club beat Bradford City 2-1 with goals from Berry (penalty) and Bamber. Facing Yorkshire opposition again in Leeds United in the second round, the Potters lost 5-4 on penalties after the game had ended all-square at 2-2.

ZIGGER ZAGGER

This is the title of Peter Terson's play about the football scene of 1967. It was taken from the chant of avid Stoke City fan, J. Bageley. Giving a view of life from the terraces, it is a rare example of football being treated as a suitable subject for the stage, and was written specifically for the National Youth Theatre. The action mixes football motifs with an examination of the bleak prospects facing a football-obsessed teenager in a society which appears to have failed him.

Index

A

abandoned matches	1
Accrington Stanley	2
Allen, Harry	108
Allen, Tony	3, 5, 20, 68
Almond, Henry	42, 114
Andrew, Ron	95
Anglo-Italian League Cup	3
Anglo-Scottish Cup	119
Archibald, Bobby	56, 81
Arsenal	66
Asprey, Bill	5, 35, 38
Austerberry, Horace	7
Austerberry, R.D.L.	16
Autoglass Trophy	48, 68

B

Baddeley, Amos	17, 94
Baddeley, George	17, 19
Bageley, J.	134
Ball, Alan	10, 76
Banks, Gordon	11, 44 - 45, 52, 61, 104 - 105, 118, 121 - 122, 129
Barker, Alfred	12, 57
Barker, Richie	6, 12, 34, 36
Barnes, Paul	29, 65, 98
Bebbington, Keith	115
Bernard, Mike	119
Bertschin, Keith	50
Biggins, Wayne	116
Bingham, Harry	64
Birch, Philip	89
Birmingham City	29, 97
Bloor, Alan	14, 33 - 34, 66, 108, 119, 122
Bolton Wanderers	32, 35, 123
Bower, Sid	55
Bowyer, Frank	16, 20, 89, 94
Bradley, Fred	26
Bradshaw, Joseph	17, 96

Broad, Jimmy	17, 21, 64, 78, 90, 120
Broad, Tommy	17
Brookes, Issac (Ike)	28
Brooks, Sammy	55
Bullock, Peter	2
Burnden Park	32
Burnley	28, 35
Burrows, Harry	119
Bury	35, 71
Butler, John	86
Buxton, Peter	16

C

Caernarfon Wanderers	14
Campbell Road	23, 37
Capes, Adrian	17
Capes, Arthur	17, 81
Cardiff City	35
Central League	19
Chamberlain, Mark	13, 18
Chamberlain, Neville	18
Charlton Athletic	35
Charnley, Tom	65
Clamp, Eddie	129
Clare, Tommy	19, 38, 89
Clough, Brian	36, 105
Coleman, Neville	53, 56
Connor, Harry	113
Conroy, Terry	26, 45, 62, 104, 119, 122
Cowlishaw W.A.	100
Cox, Walter	27
Cranston, Ian	121
Cullis, Stan	49
Cunliffe, Dickie	83

D

Davies, Harry	20 - 21, 29, 56, 78, 112, 120
Dean, Dixie	113
Dixon, Bob	24
Dobing, Peter	19, 28, 33, 116

Dodd, Alan 5, 20, 34
Dodd, Dodd 123
Donoghue, Steve 81
Dorsett, Dickie 82
Doyle, Mike 13
Durban, Alan 26, 34, 36

E

Eastham, George 45, 97
Edge, Alf 89
Elder, Alex 129
Evans, Ray 13
Evans, Ted 33, 81
Eyres, Johnny 56

F

Fairs Cup 3
Farrell, Jack 118
Fielding, Abraham 89
Football Alliance 17, 43
Football Alliance Championship 28
Football League Cup 34
Ford, Peter 83
Foster, W.J. 16
Fox, Peter 33, 48, 52
Franklin, Neil 24, 49, 83, 131

G

Gillies, Matt 105
Glasgow Rangers 57
goalkeepers 51
Graver, Andy 46
Greenhoff, Jimmy 20, 54, 98, 119, 121, 131
Gregg, Harry 67
Griffiths, Arthur 14
Griffiths, Jack 55
Grobbelaar, Bruce 48

H

Hamlett, Lol 55
Hampton, Harry 55
Hancock, Tom 102
Hargreaves, Henry 130
Haslegrave, Sean 119
Hatch, Tony 88
Heath, Adrian 13

Henshall, Albert 117
Herd, David 129
Herod, Dennis 52
Herron, Richard 81, 130
Hillier, Brian 67
Hodge, Peter 57
Hodgkins, Reg 30
Holford, Tom 5, 20, 57, 81
Howe, Tom 78
Hudson, Alan 54, 59, 121
Hurst, Geoff 28, 33, 104, 115, 121 - 122
Hurst, Rev. A.E. 52
Hyslop, Tom 30, 56, 62, 85

J

James, Charlie 85
Jennings, Pat 83
Jepson, Arthur 27
Johnson, Edward 62
Johnson, Joe 120
Johnson, Teddy 62
Jones, Roger 24
Jordan, Joe 63

K

Kearton, Jason 48
Kelly, George 81, 113
Kelly, Nyrere 115
Kelly, Tony 81
Kendall, Howard 36
King, Johnny 20, 94, 113, 133
Kinson, Tom 130
Kirton, John 19
Kroll, Ruud 122

L

Larrson, Sven 46
Lawton, Tommy 113
Lenaghan, George 56
Leyland Daf Cup 8
Leyton Orient 123
Limer, George 130
Lincoln City 19
Lockett, Harry 17, 27, 65
Lonsdale Street 23, 37
Luton Town 35

M

Macari, Lou 67
Mahoney, John 70, 85, 115
Manchester City 7
Mansfield 29
Marsh, Jackie 71, 76
Martin, Wade 16, 46
Mather, Tom 30, 72, 90, 102, 110, 122
Matthews, Stanley 2, 22, 32, 44, 66,
69, 73, 75, 95, 117, 120, 126 - 127
Matthews, Tony 16
Matthews, William Macdonald 114
Mawson, Joe 17, 90
Maxwell, Allen 120
Maxwell, Willie 75
McCormick, Bob 28
McCue, John 68
McGrory, Bob 5, 20, 27, 38, 40, 66, 69,
82, 102, 105, 110, 112
McIlroy, Jimmy 22, 91, 95, 127
McIlroy, Sammy 13
Meredith, Sammy 62
Mills, Mick 75
Moores, Ian 124, 132
Mould, Billy 121
Mountford, Edgar 17, 89
Mountford, Frank 77, 85, 131
Mountford, George 24, 49, 83
Mountford, Harry 17
Mow Cop 14
Mullard, Albert 89
Mullineux, Ernest 81
Murphy, Joe 81

N

New Ground 80
Nixon, Walter 130
North Staffords' Comfort Fund 130
North Staffordshire
League championship 28
Nottingham Forest 131

O

O'Callaghan, Brendan 31
O'Neill, Jimmy 95
Oakes, John 55

Orlygsson, Toddy 46
Oscroft, Harry 20, 56, 82

P

Page, Loius 112
Palethorpe, Jack 91
Palmer, Calvin 24
Parker, Charlie 79, 105
Parker, Garry 87
Paterson, George 30, 56
Peacock, Keith 115
Pearson, Tom 55
Pejic, Mel 18
Pejic, Mike 18, 84
Pele 84
Peschisolido, Paul 48
Player of the Year 34
Poole, Kevin 87
Port Vale 28, 42, 52, 64, 88, 132
Potts, Mike 102
Preston North End 14, 31
Proctor, John 30
Puskas, Ference 95

R

Ramsey, Bob 2, 123
Reeves, Arthur 17, 96
Revill, Tom 27
Rhodes, Bernard 89
Richardson, Paul 91
Ripley, Stan 130
Ritchie, John 20, 33, 44 - 45, 54, 83,
104, 116, 119, 122
Robinson, Jack 52
Roose, Leigh Richmond 28, 52, 62,
88, 130
Ross, Jimmy 14
Rowley, William 7, 51, 88, 98, 99
Rutherford, John 99

S

Sale, Tommy 20, 56, 82, 130 - 131
Sandford, Lee 86, 117
Saunders, Carl 115, 123
Schofield, Joe 79, 100, 118
Scrimshaw, Charlie 55
Second Division championship 31

Segers, Hans   48
Sellars, Harry   17, 39, 102 - 103
Sellars, John   39, 103, 113, 123
Setters, Maurice   24
Shallcross, Arthur   105
Shardlow, Paul   30
Shaw, Graham   86
Sheffield Wednesday   35
Sheridan, Jack   62
Sheron, Mike   54
Sherpa Van Trophy   65
Shilton, Peter   11, 52, 105, 121
Shorthouse, Jack   130
Shutt, George   89
Sigurdsson, Larus   46
Simod Cup   133
Simpkinson, Rev. C.H.   23
Skeels, Eric   66, 107, 122 - 123
Slaney, Thomas   108
Slaney, Tom   7
Smith, Denis   15, 34, 60, 108, 121 - 122
Smith, Ted   89
Smyth, Sammy   62
Soo, Frank   109
Spencer, Billy   112
Staffordshire County Cup   14
Starmer, Sir Lovelace   23
Steele, Freddie   16, 20, 54 - 56, 64, 82,
                                      113, 116
Stefano, Alfredi di   95
Stein, Mark   8, 23, 87, 121
Stephenson, Clem   29
Stoke End Stand   42
Stoke Ramblers   42, 46
Sturgess, Albert   81
Sturridge, Simon   56

T

Taylor, Frank   66, 116, 127
Terson, Peter   134
Third Division (North)
    Championship   31
Thomas, J.W.   114
Thomas, Mickey   13
Tottenham Hotspur   31
Trent, Jackie   88
Tudor, John   30

Tunnicliffe, Billy   17
Tunnicliffe, John   17
Turner, Arthur   5, 20, 38, 121
Turner, George   19

U

U.S. Soccer Association   24
Ursem, Loek   46

V

Vernon, Roy   129
Victoria Ground   18, 25, 27 - 28, 42, 61,
                              64, 78, 86, 132
Viollet, Dennis   22, 95, 115, 129

W

Waddington, Tony   34, 38, 66, 91, 98
Ward, Derek   18
Ward, Tom   30
Ward, Tony   18
Ware   17
Ware, Harry   55, 113
Ware, Paul   8, 104, 123
Watkin, Arthur   18, 89
Watkin, Frank   18
Watkins, Mart   62
West Bromwich Albion   14, 41
Westland, Doug   18
Westland, Jim   18, 56
Whitta Taylor, John   102
Williams, Dick   85
Williams, Josh   80
Wilshaw, Dennis   94
Wilson, Charlie   5, 13, 20 - 21, 53 - 54,
                              76, 90, 116, 120
Wiseman, Roger   29
Wolverhampton Wanderers   132

STOKE NOTES

Please add your favourite "A-Z" notes on these two pages and send them to us (address on back cover). We will try to include them in future editions of this book!

STOKE NOTES

More Great Books from . . .

We publish a wide range of books (currently over 200!). Some are about football, but many are for more general leisure pursuits. Here is a small selection:

COUNTRY & WESTERN LINE DANCING: Step-by-Step Instructions for Cowgirls & Cowboys

FROM OVER THERE TO OVER HERE! Written by Judy Dygdon & Anthony Conger, two American line dance teachers, this is the first book published in Britain on the new dance craze! Teach yourself the dances and amaze your friends! Brush up on your technique! There are clear step-by-step instructions for more than 50 dances, and they've all been carefully checked to be sure that they're authentic and that they all work perfectly - you'll find all the popular ones plus some more unusual dances and there's even a list at the back to remind you how to do each step. There's recommended music on a well-produced and FREE CD containing 12 tracks of Country & Western music carefully matched to the dances. Our book was so popular that it was featured in many popular newspapers and magazine, including SHE and MY WEEKLY. *£12.95*

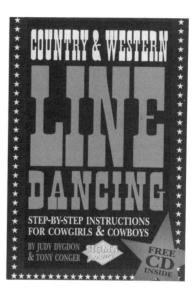

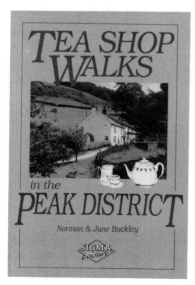

TEASHOP WALKS IN THE PEAK DISTRICT

This guidebook contains twenty-six varied and attractive walks suitable for all the family. June and Norman Buckley describe them with accurate instructions, clear sketch maps and delightful photographs. To add to the pleasure, each walk includes one or more teashops; ranging from a homely farmhouse kitchen to a converted cotton mill. The walks are spaced throughout the Peak District. There are strolls in the peaceful valleys of Dovedale, Lathkill Dale and Miller's Dale, high-level walks up Shutlingsloe, the 'Matterhorn of Cheshire', and along the Roaches, and visits to such typical Peakland towns and villages as Bakewell and Tissington. *£6.95*

BEST STAFFORDSHIRE WALKS

Les Lumsdon is a Senior Lecturer in tourism at the University of Staffordshire and knows his county like the back of his hand. He has also completely revised and up-dated his book to produce this new edition of a popular collection of country walks. £6.95

BEST PUB WALKS IN NORTH STAFFORDSHIRE

Les Lumsdon joins forces with local photographer Chris Rushton to produce this super collection of walks that are all based on popular local hostelries. Varied walks, excellent pubs and real ale all combine to make perfect days out. £6.95

BEST PUB WALKS IN SOUTH STAFFORDSHIRE

This South Staffs companion , due in 1997, completes our coverage of Staffs pub walks: discover the charm of country walks in the traditional home of real ale. £6.95

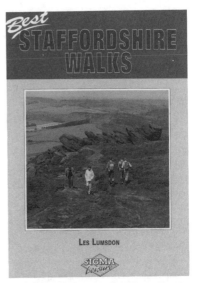

GOLF COURSES OF CHESHIRE

Mark Rowlinson

"Reminders of how many treasures have still to be visited" DAILY TELEGRAPH.

£9.95

GOLF COURSES OF NORTH WALES

Mark Rowlinson & Peter Lees

"With this book in the bag, the rest is easy" - TONY LEWIS: WALES TOURIST BOARD.

£9.95   *(April 1997)*

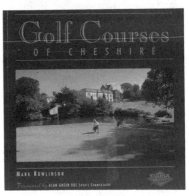

You can order our books from your local bookshop, and we also supply by mail order. Please add £2 p&p (UK).

Sigma Leisure, 1 South Oak Lane, Wilmslow, Cheshire, SK9 6AR.
Tel: 01625-531035;
Fax: 01625-536800

Our complete on-line catalogue is on the Internet:

http://www.sigmapress.co.uk